Introductory Chaldean

Bp. Sarhad Y. Jammo
Fr. Andrew Younan

Published by the Chaldean Media Center:
Chaldean Media Center, 1627 Jamacha Way, El Cajon, CA, USA

Cover design by Andrew Hermiz.

www.kaldu.org

First Edition Published in San Diego in 2014.

ISBN-13: 978-1503371163
ISBN-10: 1503371166

First Printing.

Table of Contents

Unit 5

Unit 6

Preface

Units 1-3 of this book introduce the Chaldean language by teaching letter recognition and pronunciation while building vocabulary and reading fluency skills. Note that the letters are not taught in alphabetical order, but in an order that allows one to construct words immediately.

Each chapter contains 3 sections, labeled: *Recognize*, *Read*, and *Remember*. In the **Recognize** section the letters are introduced in a pronunciation chart.

Each **Read** section teaches and reinforces proper vowel and consonant pronunciation and provides lessons to test comprehension and improve fluency. Repeating aloud the sounds of the vowel-consonant combinations as they are introduced will make it easier to pronounce the vocabulary.

The **Remember** section tests memory by translation exercises, and vocabulary is given with the transliterations (the sound of the word written in English letters), as well as the definitions. Making flash cards of the vocabulary will not only aid in memorization but also in handwriting and fluency. Although it is beneficial to learn transliterations to aid in pronunciation, it is not suggested to rely on the transliterations when memorizing the vocabulary. Therefore, try to translate each word directly from Chaldean to English first and then transliterating for extra practice. The vocabulary is deliberately repetitive throughout the book.

After every third lesson there is a **Review** of all of the vocabulary from the previous lessons. Read through the lists of vocabulary until there is no hesitation on the pronunciation of the Chaldean words or for the definitions of the words.

It is recommended to complete these exercises on a separate sheet of paper so that the lessons and activities may be repeated to improve language proficiency.

Units 4-6 of this book build on the basics and vocabulary learned in the first three units, in order for the learner to be able to begin conversing in Chaldean. Each chapter contains 5 sections:

The Language sections introduce the student to the basic grammar of the Chaldean language, and prepare him for the comprehensive study of grammar in the next book in this series.

Typical conversations in the Chaldean language illustrate the grammar and vocabulary, and challenge the student to analyze the structure of the language in its practical applications.

This section introduces (or re-introduces) some of the words and expressions used in the dialogue. The words will be both translated and transliterated in order to aid with pronunciation.

This section tests comprehension of the material with Exercises that require translation, answering questions or forming phrases.

This last section highlights a particular area of Chaldean culture as it is related to the material learned in the chapter. These brief sections can provide a unique look into the culture for those who may not be familiar with Chaldean culture or its history.

Pronunciation

Name	As in...	Transliteration	Consonant
Alap	<u>a</u>ir	`	ܐ
Beth	<u>b</u>oy	b	ܒ
Gamal	<u>g</u>irl	g	ܓ
Dalath	<u>d</u>og	d	ܕ
Heh	<u>h</u>ello	h	ܗ
Waw	<u>w</u>ow	w	ܘ
Zayn	<u>z</u>ip	z	ܙ
<u>*H*</u>*eth*	(guttural h)	<u>h</u>	ܚ
<u>*T*</u>*eth*	(guttural t)	<u>t</u>	ܛ
Yodh	<u>y</u>ou	y	ܝ
Kap	<u>c</u>at	k	ܟ
Lamadh	<u>l</u>ove	l	ܠ
Mym	<u>m</u>om	m	ܡ
Nun	<u>n</u>ame	n	ܢ
Simkath	<u>s</u>ip	s	ܣ
'e	(guttural e)	'	ܥ
Pe	<u>p</u>en	p	ܦ
<u>*S*</u>*ade*	(guttural s)	<u>s</u>	ܨ
Qop	<u>q</u>uilt	q	ܩ
Resh	<u>r</u>ed	r	ܪ
Shyn	<u>sh</u>eep	sh	ܫ
Taw	<u>t</u>ent	t	ܬ

These phrases are an easy way to memorize the 22 consonants:

ܒܬܥܥ	ܣܥܩܝ	ܟܠܡܢ	ܚܛܝ	ܗܘܘܙ	ܐܒܓܕ
Qar-shat	Sa'pas	Kol-man	Hat-ty	Haw-waz	Abgad

Vowels

Traditionally, written Chaldean did not have any vowels. A system of dots was later developed to accompany the words and distinguish the appropriate vowel vocalizations. The dotted circle represents where the letter would be placed.

Name	As in...	Transliteration	Vowel
Zqapa	ball	a	
Zlama Kirya	bit	i	
Pthaha	balloon	a	
Zlama Qishya	bear	e	
Waw Rwykhta	boat	o	ܘ
Waw 'yqta	boot	u	ܘ
Hwasa	beet	y	

Modified Letters

According to the classic Chaldean grammar, 6 of the consonants admit modification or alteration to produce 6 new consonants.

Name	As in...	Transliteration	Letter
Weth	wow	w	ܒ
Ghamal	(softened g)	gh	ܓ
Dhalath	the	dh	ܕ
Khap	Bach	kh	ܟ
Phe	phone or wow	ph or w	ܦ
Thaw	thick	th	ܬ

Additional Consonants

In order to meet the needs of modern Chaldean, other modifications have been introduced for the sake of additional sounds. The symbol is placed below the letter to produce the new pronunciation. Only *Beth*, *Gamal*, *Ṭeth*, and *Kap* accept this kind of modification.

Name	As in...	Transliteration	Letter
Veth	v̱ery	v	ܒ
Jamal	ǰazz	j	ܓ
Dthe	(guttural ṯ)	dth	ܛ
Chap	c̱hop	ch	ܟ

Final Forms and Connecting Letters

As noted in the chart, three of the consonants have **final forms**: *Kap*, *Mym* and *Nun*. The final form of *Mym* is always the same: ܡ, whereas *Kap* and *Nun* differ depending on whether they are attached or unattached to the previous letter:

ܟ ܗ

ܢ ܗ

It is quite easy to tell whether a letter attaches to the one which follows it: if the part of the letter that is on the "writing line" is longer than the rest of the letter, then it connects to the next letter; otherwise, it does not. So, the letters that connect are: *Beth*, *Gamal*, *Ḥeth*, *Ṭeth*, *Yodh*, *Kap*, *Lamadh*, *Mym*, *Nun*, *Simkath*, *'e*, *Pe*, *Qop* and *Shyn*; those that do not connect are: *Alap*, *Dalath*, *Heh*, *Waw*, *Zayn*, *Ṣade*, *Resh* and *Taw*. The combination, at the end of a word, between *Taw* and *Alap*, has a special form: ܬܐ.

Mbatlana and *Syame*

At times a letter may go unpronounced, in which case a *mbatlana* (a thin line above or below the unpronounced letter) is used, as in: ‫ܐ‬‫ܚܬܐ‬ ، ‫ܡܕܝ݂ܢܬܐ‬.

Finally, there are grammatical marks that are used to show the number or tense of the word, such as *Syame*, which indicate the plural: ܸ ، ܿ.

Writing the Consonants

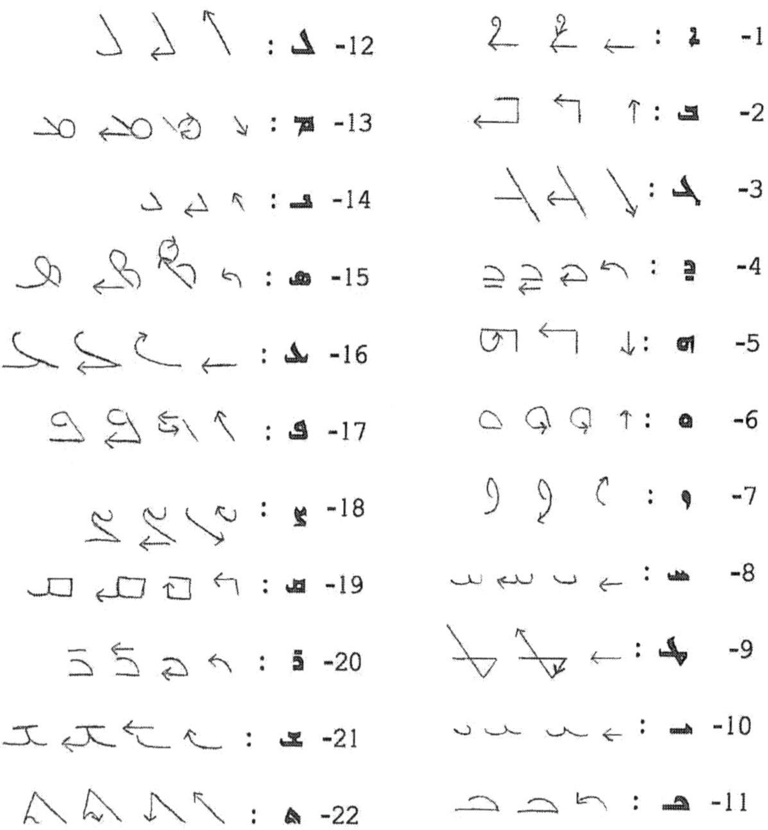

‫ܠ‬ ‫ܠ‬ ‫ܠ‬	: ‫ܠ‬ -12			‫ܐ‬ ‫ܐ‬ ‫ܐ‬	: ‫ܐ‬ -1
‫ܡ‬ ‫ܡ‬ ‫ܡ‬ ‫ܡ‬	: ‫ܡ‬ -13			‫ܒ‬ ‫ܒ‬ ‫ܒ‬	: ‫ܒ‬ -2
‫ܢ‬ ‫ܢ‬ ‫ܢ‬	: ‫ܢ‬ -14			‫ܓ‬ ‫ܓ‬ ‫ܓ‬	: ‫ܓ‬ -3
‫ܣ‬ ‫ܣ‬ ‫ܣ‬ ‫ܣ‬	: ‫ܣ‬ -15			‫ܕ‬ ‫ܕ‬ ‫ܕ‬ ‫ܕ‬	: ‫ܕ‬ -4
‫ܥ‬ ‫ܥ‬ ‫ܥ‬ ‫ܥ‬	: ‫ܥ‬ -16			‫ܗ‬ ‫ܗ‬ ‫ܗ‬	: ‫ܗ‬ -5
‫ܦ‬ ‫ܦ‬ ‫ܦ‬ ‫ܦ‬	: ‫ܦ‬ -17			‫ܘ‬ ‫ܘ‬ ‫ܘ‬	: ‫ܘ‬ -6
‫ܨ‬ ‫ܨ‬ ‫ܨ‬	: ‫ܨ‬ -18			‫ܙ‬ ‫ܙ‬ ‫ܙ‬	: ‫ܙ‬ -7
‫ܩ‬ ‫ܩ‬ ‫ܩ‬ ‫ܩ‬	: ‫ܩ‬ -19			‫ܚ‬ ‫ܚ‬ ‫ܚ‬ ‫ܚ‬	: ‫ܚ‬ -8
‫ܪ‬ ‫ܪ‬ ‫ܪ‬ ‫ܪ‬	: ‫ܪ‬ -20			‫ܛ‬ ‫ܛ‬ ‫ܛ‬	: ‫ܛ‬ -9
‫ܫ‬ ‫ܫ‬ ‫ܫ‬ ‫ܫ‬	: ‫ܫ‬ -21			‫ܝ‬ ‫ܝ‬ ‫ܝ‬ ‫ܝ‬	: ‫ܝ‬ -10
‫ܬ‬ ‫ܬ‬ ‫ܬ‬ ‫ܬ‬	: ‫ܬ‬ -22			‫ܟ‬ ‫ܟ‬ ‫ܟ‬	: ‫ܟ‬ -11

Chapter 1

In this chapter, six letters are introduced: *Alap, Beth, Dalath, Lamadh, Mym* and *Resh*, as well as two vowel marks: long *a* and *i*. Note that *Mym* has a "final" form.

Recognize

Name	As in...	Transliteration	Consonant
Alap	<u>a</u>ir	`	ܐ
Beth	<u>b</u>oy	b	ܒ
Dalath	<u>d</u>og	d	ܕ
Lamadh	<u>l</u>ove	l	ܠ
Mym	<u>m</u>om	m	ܡ ، ܡ
Resh	<u>r</u>ed	r	ܪ

Name	As in...	Transliteration	Vowel
Zqapa	b<u>a</u>ll	a	ܿ
Zlama Kirya	b<u>i</u>t	i	ܸ

The chart below is to demonstrate how to read consonants when they are accompanied by a vowel. Note that the letter *Alap* does not have a sound on its own, and is essentially a "vowel-carrier."

sound	+ i	sound	+ long a	Consonant
i	ܐ	a	ܐ	ܐ
bi	ܒ	ba	ܒ	ܒ
di	ܕ	da	ܕ	ܕ
li	ܠ	la	ܠ	ܠ

1

Read

A.

Read each line below from right to left to practice the vowel and consonant combinations. Reading the letters out loud will aid in memorizing the vowel sounds and improve fluency.

1. ܐ ܐ ܐ ، ܐܵ ܐܵ ܐܵ ، ܐܹ ܐܹ ܐܹ
2. ܒ ܒ ܒ ، ܒܵ ܒܵ ܒܵ ، ܒܹ ܒܹ ܒܹ، ܒܵܒܵܐ ܒܵܒܵܐ ܒܵܒܵܐ
3. ܕ ܕ ܕ ، ܕܵ ܕܵ ܕܵ ، ܕܹ ܕܹ ܕܹ ، ܕܵܕܵܐ ܕܵܕܵܐ ܕܵܕܵܐ ، ܕܹܒܵܐ ܕܹܒܵܐ ܕܹܒܵܐ
4. ܠ ܠ ܠ ، ܠܵ ܠܵ ܠܵ ، ܠܹ ܠܹ ܠܹ ، ܠܹܒܵܐ ܠܹܒܵܐ ܠܹܒܵܐ
5. ܡ ܡ ܡ ، ܡܵ ܡܵ ܡܵ ، ܡܹ ܡܹ ܡܹ ، ܡܵܡܵܐ ܡܵܡܵܐ ܡܵܡܵܐ
6. ܪ ܪ ܪ ، ܪܵ ܪܵ ܪܵ ، ܪܹ ܪܹ ܪܹ ، ܪܵܒܵܐ ܪܵܒܵܐ ܪܵܒܵܐ

B.

Read the following lines out loud, repeating as necessary until they can be read with ease. For extra practice, translate each line into English.

1. ܒܵܒܵܐ، ܕܵܕܵܐ، ܪܵܒܵܐ، ܪܵܡܵܐ، ܒܵܒܵܐ، ܪܵܒܵܐ، ܕܵܕܵܐ، ܪܵܡܵܐ
2. ܡܵܡܵܐ، ܡܵܪܵܐ، ܐܹܠܵܐ، ܡܹܠܵܠܵܐ، ܡܵܪܵܐ، ܡܹܠܵܠܵܐ، ܡܵܡܵܐ
3. ܕܹܒܵܐ، ܕܹܡܵܐ، ܕܠܵܐ، ܠܵܐ، ܠܹܒܵܐ، ܠܹܒܵܒܵܐ، ܕܹܒܵܐ، ܠܹܒܵܐ، ܕܹܡܵܐ، ܠܹܒܵܒܵܐ
4. ܡܹܐ، ܡܵܐ، ܐܹܠܵܐ، ܠܵܐ، ܕܹܒܵܐ، ܕܠܵܐ، ܪܵܡܵܐ، ܡܵܡܵܐ، ܪܵܒܵܐ

Remember

Meaning	Sound	Word	Meaning	Sound	Word
heart	libba	ܠܸܒܵܐ	but; yet	illa	ܐܸܠܵܐ
bold	libbana	ܠܸܒܵܢܵܐ	father	baba	ܒܵܒܵܐ
What?	ma	ܡܵܐ	of	d	ܕ
mother	mama	ܡܵܡܵܐ	dear kid	dada	ܕܵܕܵܐ
lord	mara	ܡܵܪܵܐ	bear	dibba	ܕܸܒܵܐ
fulness	milaa	ܡܸܠܵܐ	blood	dimma	ܕܸܡܵܐ
from	min	ܡܼܢ	without	dla	ܕܠܵܐ
great	raba	ܪܵܒܵܐ	to	l	ܠ
high	rama	ܪܵܡܵܐ	no	la	ܠܵܐ

Exercises

A.

Translate the following Chaldean words into English. For extra practice, transliterate each line as well.

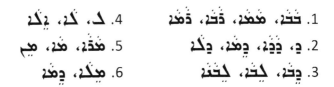

4. ܠ، ܠܵܐ، ܒܸܠܵܐ

5. ܪܵܒܵܐ، ܡܵܐ، ܡܼܢ

6. ܡܸܠܵܐ، ܕܸܡܵܐ

1. ܒܸܠܵܐ، ܡܵܡܵܐ، ܪܵܒܵܐ، ܕܸܡܵܐ

2. ܕ، ܕܵܕܵܐ، ܕܸܡܵܐ، ܒܸܠܵܐ

3. ܕܸܒܵܐ، ܠܸܒܵܐ، ܠܸܒܵܢܵܐ

B.

Translate the following English words into Chaldean.

1. bear, blood, but
2. father, mother, to
3. heart, hearty, high

4. what, no, from
5. master, great, bold
6. fulness, of, without

Chapter 2

Three letters are introduced, *Kap*, *Nun*, and *Shyn*, along with three vowel marks, *a*, *o* and *u*. The letters and vowels learned from Chapter 1 will be used with these new letters to form the vocabulary for this lesson.

Recognize

Name	As in...	Transliteration	Consonant
Kap	<u>c</u>at	k	ܟ
Nun	<u>n</u>ame	n	ܢ
Shyn	<u>sh</u>eep	sh	ܫ

Remember that *Kap* and *Nun* have final forms:

Attached	Detached	Consonant
ܟ	ܟ	ܟ
ܢ	ܢ	ܢ

The vowels for this Chapter:

Name	As in...	Transliteration	Vowel
Pthaha	b<u>a</u>lloon	a	ܲ
Waw Rwykhta	b<u>oa</u>t	o	ܘ̇
Waw 'yqta	b<u>oo</u>t	u	ܘ̣

Again, here is a chart to illustrate how these new vowels work with consonants. Of course, any consonant can be combined with any vowel, and you will have to combine them on your own from this point on.

sound	+ *u*	sound	+ *o*	Consonant
ku	ܟܘܼ	*ko*	ܟܘܿ	ܟ
nu	ܢܘܼ	*no*	ܢܘܿ	ܢ
shu	ܫܘܼ	*sho*	ܫܘܿ	ܫ

Read

A.

Read each line below from right to left to practice the vowel and consonant combinations.

1. ܟ ܟ ܟ ، ܟܵ ܟܵ ܟܵ ، ܟܹ ܟܹ ܟܹ ، ܟܲ ܟܲ ܟܲ ،
ܟܵܟܵܐ، ܟܹܐܦܵܐ، ܡܲܠܟܵܐ، ܟܲܪܡܵܐ، ܟܲܠܬܵܐ

2. ܢ ܢ ܢ ، ܢܵ ܢܵ ܢܵ ، ܢܹ ܢܹ ܢܹ ، ܢܲ ܢܲ ܢܲ ، ܢܘܿ ܢܘܿ ܢܘܿ ،
ܢܘܼ ܢܘܼ ܢܘܼ ، ܢܹܫܪܵܐ، ܟܹܢܵܪܵܐ، ܟܪܘܿܢܵܐ، ܪܘܼܡܵܐ، ܟܘܿܡܵܐ، ܟܘܼܡܵܐ،
ܢܘܼܪܵܐ

3. ܫ ܫ ܫ ، ܫܵ ܫܵ ܫܵ ، ܫܹ ܫܹ ܫܹ ، ܫܲ ܫܲ ܫܲ ،
ܫܘܿ ܫܘܿ ܫܘܿ ، ܫܘܼ ܫܘܼ ܫܘܼ ، ܫܹܡܵܐ، ܫܹܡܫܵܐ، ܫܠܵܡܵܐ،
ܫܲܡܵܫܵܐ، ܠܘܼܫܵܫܵܐ

B.

Read the following lines out loud, repeating as necessary until they can be read with ease.

1. ܐܒܘܢܐ، ܒܘܡܐ، ܟܘܡܐ، ܐܒܘܢܐ، ܒܪܢܫܐ، ܟܘܡܐ، ܡܠܟܐ
2. ܒܫ، ܒܘܫܠܐ، ܒܘܪܟܐ، ܒܪܢܫܐ، ܒܘܫܠܐ، ܒܘܪܟܐ، ܒܪܢܫܐ
3. ܕܒܫܐ، ܕܪܡܢܐ، ܐܟܪܐ، ܟܢܪܐ، ܠܘܫܢܐ، ܒܪܢܫܐ، ܕܪܫܐ، ܐܢܐ
4. ܟܡܐ، ܟܟܐ، ܟܘܡܐ، ܢܫܠܐ، ܪܘܡܐ، ܪܢܕܐ، ܪܡܫܐ
5. ܪܘܡܐ، ܒܪܢܫܐ، ܒܘܡܐ، ܪܘܡܐ، ܕܒܫܐ ܒܒܪܘܡܐ، ܡܠܟܐ ܟܢܐ
6. ܢܡܪܐ ܒܪܢܫܐ، ܕܪܡܢܐ، ܢܢܐ ܒܢܫܠܐ، ܡܠܟܐ ܟܘܡܐ

Remember

Meaning	Sound	Word	Meaning	Sound	Word
just	*kena*	ܟܢܐ	Father	*abuna*	ܐܒܘܢܐ
mouth	*kimma*	ܟܡܐ	farmer	*akkara*	ܐܟܪܐ
harp	*kinnara*	ܟܢܪܐ	I	*ana*	ܐܢܐ
black	*koma*	ܟܘܡܐ	in	*b*	ܒ
tongue	*lushana*	ܠܘܫܢܐ	son of	*bar*	ܒܪ
king	*malka*	ܡܠܟܐ	man	*barnasha*	ܒܪܢܫܐ
grandma	*nana*	ܢܢܐ	more	*bish*	ܒܫ
tiger	*nimra*	ܢܡܪܐ	knee	*burka*	ܒܘܪܟܐ
eagle	*nishra*	ܢܫܪܐ	meal	*bushala*	ܒܘܫܠܐ
monk	*rabban*	ܪܒܢ	owl	*buma*	ܒܘܡܐ
evening	*ramsha*	ܪܡܫܐ	bee	*dabasha*	ܕܒܫܐ
good	*randa*	ܪܢܕܐ	medicine	*darmana*	ܕܪܡܢܐ
hill	*roma*	ܪܘܡܐ	enemy	*dishmin*	ܕܫܡܢ

picture	*shikla*	ܫܟܠܐ	study	*drasha*	ܕܪܫܐ
name	*shimma*	ܫܡܐ	tooth	*kaka*	ܟܟܐ
sun	*shimsha*	ܫܡܫܐ	dog	*kalba*	ܟܠܒܐ
peace	*shlama*	ܫܠܡܐ	angry	*karbana*	ܟܪܒܢܐ
date	*tumra*	ܬܘܡܪܐ	vineyard	*karma*	ܟܪܡܐ

Exercises

A.

Translate the following Chaldean words into English. For extra practice, transliterate each line as well.

1. ܒܪܐ، ܒܝܬ، ܐܒܐ، ܒܒܐ، ܓܒܢܐ
2. ܕܪܡܢܐ، ܟܪܒܢܐ، ܝܫܪܐ
3. ܡܠܟܐ، ܫܟܠܐ، ܫܠܡܐ
4. ܒܘܡܐ، ܒܘܪܟܐ، ܟܠܒܐ
5. ܪܘܡܐ، ܐܟܪܐ، ܐܒܘܢܐ، ܐܢܐ
6. ܫܡܫܐ، ܝܡܪܐ، ܟܪܡܐ
7. ܟܪܢܫܐ، ܒܘܫܠܐ، ܠܘܫܢܐ
8. ܒܡܐ، ܫܡܐ، ܟܟܐ، ܪܒܝ

B.

Translate the following English words into Chaldean.

1. bee, dog, tiger, eagle
2. farmer, son, man, grandma
3. monk, picture, sun
4. just, good, tongue
5. tooth, mouth, name
6. enemy, angry, black
7. harp, evening, peace
8. I, in, more, meal

Chapter 3

In this chapter, three more consonants are introduced, *Gamal*, *Taw* and *Waw*. Again, letters and vowels from previous lessons will be incorporated into these new vocabulary words.

Recognize

Name	As in...	Transliteration	Consonant
Gamal	girl	*g*	ܓ
Taw	<u>t</u>ent	*t*	ܬ
Waw	<u>w</u>ow	*w*	ܘ

Read

A.
Read each line below from right to left.

1. ܓ ܓ ܓ ، ܓܵ ܓܵ ܓܵ ، ܓܹ ܓܹ ܓܹ ، ܓܲ ܓܲ ܓܲ ، ܓܘܿ ܓܘܿ ܓܘܿ ، ܓܘܼ ܓܘܼ ܓܘܼ ، ܓܘܼܕܵܐ، ܓܘܼܡܠܵܐ، ܓܲܒܵܪܵܐ، ܓܲܒܵܪܘܿܬܵܐ

2. ܬ ܬ ܬ ، ܬܵ ܬܵ ܬܵ ، ܬܹ ܬܹ ܬܹ ، ܬܲ ܬܲ ܬܲ ، ܬܘܿ ܬܘܿ ܬܘܿ ، ܬܘܼ ܬܘܼ ܬܘܼ ، ܬܘܿܕܵܐ، ܬܵܡܵܐ، ܓܘܼܒܬܵܐ، ܬܘܼܡܵܕܵܐ، ܒܲܬܵܐ

3. ܘ ܘ ܘ ، ܘܵ ܘܵ ܘܵ ، ܘܹ ܘܹ ܘܹ ، ܘܲ ܘܲ ܘܲ ، ܘܘܿ ܘܘܿ ܘܘܿ ، ܘܘܼ ܘܘܼ ܘܘܼ ، ܘܲܪܕܵܐ، ܘܲܪܕܹܐ، ܒܵܘܼܬܵܐ ܘܒܲܬܵܐ، ܘܹܠܬܵܐ ܒܘܿܡܒܵܐ.

B.

Read the following lines out loud.

1. ܬܘܡܐ، ܬܡܠ، ܬܐ، ܬܘܡܪܐ، ܬܠܓܐ، ܬܡܠ، ܬܡܐ
2. ܒܪܬܐ، ܒܪܘܢܐ، ܓܪܘܡܐ، ܓܪܡܐ، ܒܪܬܐ
3. ܡܘܠܟܢܐ، ܢܘܓܐ، ܢܘܪܐ، ܬܘܡܪܐ، ܟܘܡܬܐ
4. ܓܘܡܠܐ، ܓܠܐ، ܓܪܡܐ، ܘܪܕܐ، ܕܘܪܐ، ܕܘܟܐ
5. ܒܪܬܐ ܘܒܪܘܢܐ، ܢܘܓܐ ܘܢܘܓܬܐ، ܬܘܪܬܐ ܘܬܘܪܐ
6. ܡܘܠܟܢܐ ܬܐ ܒܪܬܐ، ܐܪܡܘܢܬܐ ܬܐ ܪܒܢܬܐ

Remember

Meaning	Sound	Word	Meaning	Sound	Word
black (f)	*komta*	ܟܘܡܬܐ	pomegranate	*armonta*	ܐܪܡܘܢܬܐ
promise	*mulkana*	ܡܘܠܟܢܐ	son	*brona*	ܒܪܘܢܐ
grandson	*nawaga*	ܢܘܓܐ	daughter; girl	*brata*	ܒܪܬܐ
fire	*nura*	ܢܘܪܐ	wall	*guda*	ܓܘܕܐ
nun	*rabbanta*	ܪܒܢܬܐ	camel	*gumla*	ܓܘܡܠܐ
to; for	*ta*	ܬܐ	hay; grass	*gilla*	ܓܠܐ
garlic	*tuma*	ܬܘܡܐ	bone	*garma*	ܓܪܡܐ
date	*tumra*	ܬܘܡܪܐ	rolling pin	*garoma*	ܓܪܘܡܐ
cow	*tawirta*	ܬܘܪܬܐ	place	*duka*	ܕܘܟܐ
bull	*tora*	ܬܘܪܐ	age	*dara*	ܕܪܐ
snow	*talga*	ܬܠܓܐ	and	*w*	ܘ
there	*tama*	ܬܡܐ	rose	*warda*	ܘܪܕܐ
yesterday	*timmal*	ܬܡܠ	black	*koma*	ܟܘܡܐ

Exercises

A.

Translate the following Chaldean words into English.

1. ܬܐ، ܒܪܬܐ، ܪܒܝܥܬܐ
2. ܬܘܪܬܐ، ܢܘܟܪܐ، ܬܘܡܐ
3. ܪܡܘܢܬܐ، ܘ، ܚܘܡܢܬܐ
4. ܬܠܓܐ، ܓܘܡܠܐ، ܓܝܠܐ
5. ܬܡܐ، ܡܘܠܚܢܐ، ܬܘܪܐ
6. ܒܪܘܢܐ، ܢܘܪܐ، ܓܘܪܐ
7. ܘܪܕܐ، ܓܪܘܡܐ، ܓܪܡܐ،
8. ܬܡܠ، ܬܘܡܪܐ، ܕܘܟܐ

B.

Translate the following English words into Chaldean.

1. Rose, girl, promise
2. Cow, camel, hay, bull
3. Pomegranate, garlic, date
4. Bone, fire, rolling pin
5. Wall, room, there, to
6. Yesterday, sleep, black
7. Grandson, son, age
8. Snow, nun, came, and

Unit 1 Review

Match each word to its translation:

from	ܚܘܿܗܿܪ
tooth	ܕܘܿܡܿܪ
hair	ܠܚܘܿܪܪ
wall	ܗܘܿܕܿܡܿܪ
hill	ܡܝܢ
man	ܚܕܢܬܪ
tongue	ܚܚܪ
cow	ܠܬܢܪ
tiger	ܠܘܿܡܠܪ
camel	ܠܪ
eagle	ܝܡܕܪ
no	ܥܠܡܪ
just	ܒܘܿܪܪ
own	ܚܘܿܡܪ
fire	ܚܪܢܪ
peace	ܝܥܕܪ
place	ܕܘܿܚܪ
bee	ܕܬܪ
bear	ܗܚܡܪ
mouth	ܕܬܢܪ
monk	ܚܡܪ
mother	ܕܬ

11

Chapter 4

Chapter 4 introduces the consonants *Yodh* and *T̲eth*. *T̲eth* is the first guttural consonant introduced. "Guttural" means "pronounced in the throat." All guttural consonants are noted in the transliteration with an underline.

Recognize

Name	As in...	Transliteration	Consonant
T̲eth	(guttural t)	t̲	ܛ
Yodh	y̲ou	*y*	ܝ

Yodh, like the English letter Y, can be used both as a consonant and a vowel. The *Yodh* takes on the vowel sound when a dot is added underneath it:

Name	As in...	Transliteration	Vowel
H̲was̲a	be̲e̲t	*y*	ܝܼ

Read

A.

1. ܝ ܝ ܝ ، ܝܵ ܝܵ ܝܵ ، ܝܹ ܝܹ ܝܹ ، ܝܲ ܝܲ ܝܲ ، ܝܘܿ ܝܘܿ ܝܘܿ ،

ܝܘܼ ܝܘܼ ܝܘܼ ، ܝܘܼܡܵܐ، ܝܘܿܡܵܐ، ܡܵܝܵܐ، ܝܵܡܵܐ، ܝܲܡܵܐ، ܒܲܝܬܵܐ، ܒܹܝܬܵܐ،

ܕܘܼܝܵܐ، ܒܵܝܬܵܐ، ܒܲܝܬܵܐ

ܝܼ ܝܼ ܝܼ ، ܕܝܼܡܵܐ، ܐܝܼܬܵܐ، ܠܝܼܬܵܐ، ܐܲܝܼܕܵܐ، ܚܲܠܝܼܒܵܐ، ܕܵܝܼܒ

2. ܛ ܛ ܛ ، ܛܵ ܛܵ ܛܵ ، ܛܹ ܛܹ ܛܹ ، ܛܲ ܛܲ ܛܲ ،

ܛܘܿ ܛܘܿ ܛܘܿ ، ܛܘܼ ܛܘܼ ܛܘܼ ، ܛܝܼ ܛܝܼ ܛܝܼ ،

ܒܲܛܵܐ، ܛܲܠܝܼ، ܛܝܼܡܵܐ، ܡܵܕܛܝܼܡܵܐ، ܛܘܼܒܵܐ، ܛܝܼܒܵܐ

B.

1. ܡܛܪܐ، ܡܝܐ، ܡܢܕܝ، ܡܪ ܛܝܡܐ، ܛܝܢܐ، ܛܝܪܐ، ܛܘܪܐ
2. ܐܝܪ، ܐܡܝܪܐ، ܐܝܠܢܐ، ܒܝܫܐ، ܕܠܝܠܐ، ܟܠܝܠܐ، ܒܝܫܐ
3. ܫܘܝܬܐ، ܫܡܝܐ، ܫܡܫܐ، ܬܢܝܢܐ، ܬܪܝܢܐ، ܫܡܝܐ، ܫܘܝܬܐ
4. ܝܘܡܐ، ܝܘܢܐ، ܝܡܐ، ܝܡܐ، ܡܢܕܝ، ܪܒܝ، ܠܝܪܐ
5. ܒܪܝܐ ܘܓܘܝܐ، ܕܝܟܐ ܕܠܝܠܐ، ܬܢܝܢܐ ܒܝܫܐ
6. ܕܘܢܝܐ، ܒܛܐ ܘܛܝܪܐ، ܐܡܝܪܐ ܟܠܕܝܐ

Remember

Meaning	Sound	Word	Meaning	Sound	Word
sea	*yama*	ܝܡܐ	prince	*amyra*	ܐܡܝܪܐ
mother	*yimma*	ܝܡܐ	tree	*`ylana*	ܐܝܠܢܐ
day	*yawma*	ܝܘܡܐ	May	*`yar*	ܐܝܪ
dove	*yawna*	ܝܘܢܐ	evil	*bysha*	ܒܝܫܐ
Chaldean	*kaldaya*	ܟܠܕܝܐ	calamity	*balaya*	ܒܠܝܐ
crown	*klyla*	ܟܠܝܠܐ	outside	*barayi*	ܒܪܝܐ
coins	*lyri*	ܠܝܪܐ	duck	*batta*	ܒܛܐ
rain	*mitra*	ܡܛܪܐ	inside	*gawaya*	ܓܘܝܐ
water	*maya*	ܡܝܐ	world	*dunyi*	ܕܘܢܝܐ
thing	*mindy*	ܡܢܕܝ	rooster	*dyka*	ܕܝܟܐ
valuable	*mar tyma*	ܡܪ ܛܝܡܐ	small	*dalyla*	ܕܠܝܠܐ
teacher	*raby*	ܪܒܝ	mountain	*tura*	ܛܘܪܐ
heaven	*shmayya*	ܫܡܝܐ	value	*tyma*	ܛܝܡܐ
deacon	*shamasha*	ܫܡܫܐ	mud	*tyna*	ܛܝܢܐ
dragon	*tannyna*	ܬܢܝܢܐ	bird	*tayra*	ܛܝܪܐ
second	*trayyana*	ܬܪܝܢܐ	for me	*taly*	ܛܠܝ

Exercises

A.

Translate the following Chaldean words into English.

B.

Translate the following English words into Chaldean.

1. water, rain, sea
2. world, mountain, tree, day
3. teacher, for me, outside
4. price, coins, thing

5. rooster, bird, dove
6. dragon, calamity, evil
7. heaven, deacon, Chaldean
8. prince, crown, hand

Chapter 5

The letters *Zayn*, *Pe* and *Simkath* are introduced in Chapter 5, along with the long *e* vowel sound.

Recognize

Name	As in...	Transliteration	Consonant
Zayn	<u>z</u>ip	*z*	ܙ
Pe	<u>p</u>en	*p*	ܦ
Simkath	<u>s</u>ip	*s*	ܣ

Name	As in...	Transliteration	Vowel
Zlama Qishya	b<u>ea</u>r	*e*	◌ܹ

Read

A.

1. ܙ ܙ ܙ ، ܙܵ ܙܵ ܙܵ ، ܙܹ ܙܹ ܙܹ ، ܙܲ ܙܲ ܙܲ ، ܙܘܿ ܙܘܿ ܙܘܿ ، ܙܘܼ ܙܘܼ ܙܘܼ،

ܙܝܼ ܙܝܼ ܙܝܼ ، ܙܘܿܪܵܢܵܐ، ܙܡܵܪܵܐ، ܙܢܒܵܪܵܐ، ܙܹܡܘܿܪܬܵܐ، ܚܒܘܿܙܵܐ

2. ܦ ܦ ܦ ، ܦܵ ܦܵ ܦܵ ، ܦܹ ܦܹ ܦܹ ، ܦܲ ܦܲ ܦܲ ، ܦܘܿ ܦܘܿ ܦܘܿ،

ܦܘܼ ܦܘܼ ܦܘܼ ، ܦܝܼ ܦܝܼ ܦܝܼ ، ܦܵܦܵܐ، ܣܘܼܠܦܵܢܵܐ، ܡܲܠܦܵܢܵܐ، ܕܹܦܹܐ،

ܦܹܕܘܿܠܵܐ، ܦܝܼܠܵܐ، ܦܠܝܼܛܵܐ

❖ ܕܹ ، ܒܹ، ܦܹ، ܛܹ، ܒܹ، ܠܹ

ܕܹܢܵܐ، ܒܹܦܵܐ، ܦܹܕܵܐ، ܛܹܒܵܪܵܐ، ܒܹܪܵܐ، ܠܹܒܠܹܐ، ܛܹܒܹܐ

B.

Remember

Meaning	Sound	Word	Meaning	Sound	Word
silver	sema	ܗܙܡܐ	tasty	bassyma	ܬܗܝܡܐ
sword	seypa	ܗܝܣܦܐ	well; pit	bera	ܕܝܪܐ
go	sy	ܗܒ	spilled	byza	ܚܒܘܝ
horse	susa	ܗܘܗܐ	nearby	gebid	ܠܬܘܝ
Pope	papa	ܦܦܐ	cheese	gupta	ܠܘܩܐ
fruit	pera	ܦܝܕܐ	singer	zamara	ܘܡܐ
elephant	pyla	ܦܝܠܐ	black bird	zanzyra	ܘܢܘܒܐ
bent	plyma	ܦܠܝܡܐ	song	zimmorta	ܘܡܗܕܐ
steel	prizla	ܦܪܙܠܐ	flute	zorna	ܘܦܕܢܐ
shelf	rapi	ܕܦܝ	teaching	yulpana	ܝܘܠܦܢܐ

16

rice	*rizza*	ܪܸܙܵܐ	rock	*kepa*	ܟܹܐܦܵܐ
head	*resha*	ܪܹܫܵܐ	hair	*kosa*	ܟܘܿܣܵܐ
date	*tumra*	ܬܘܼܡܪܵܐ	night	*layli*	ܠܸܠܝܵܐ
brown	*tumrana*	ܬܘܼܡܪܵܢܵܐ	teacher	*malpana*	ܡܲܠܦܵܢܵܐ

Exercises

A.

Translate the following Chaldean words into English.

1. ܟܹܐܦܵܐ، ܣܲܝܦܵܐ، ܦܲܪܙܠܵܐ، ܟܸܣܦܵܐ
2. ܡܲܠܦܵܢܵܐ، ܙܵܡܪܵܢܵܐ، ܬܘܼܡܪܵܢܵܐ
3. ܙܡܘܼܪܬܵܐ، ܠܘܼܦܬܵܐ، ܡܘܼܠܦܵܢܵܐ
4. ܣܹܦܵܐ، ܠܸܠܝܵܐ، ܪܹܫܵܐ، ܠܸܒܹܒ
5. ܣܒ، ܦܝܼܠܵܐ، ܦܠܝܼܛܵܐ، ܙܒܘܼܢܬܵܐ
6. ܪܦܵܐ، ܪܸܙܵܐ، ܦܪܘܼܠܵܐ
7. ܣܘܼܣܵܐ، ܦܲܦܵܐ، ܒܘܼܫܠܵܐ، ܟܘܿܣܵܐ
8. ܙܡܲܪܬܵܐ، ܒܝܘܵܐ، ܚܣܝܼܡܵܐ

B.

Translate the following English words into Chaldean.

1. teacher, singer, Pope
2. silver, steel, sword, rock
3. thank you, go, nearby
4. night, well, shelf, bent
5. spilled, head, hair, brown
6. elephant, black bird, horse
7. fruit, rice, meal, cheese
8. flute, song, teaching

Chapter 6

Lesson 6 introduces the consonants *He*, *Qop* and *Sade*. *Sade* should not be confused with *Simkath*, which was learned in the previous lesson, because the emphasis here is on the guttural pronunciation.

Recognize

Name	As in...	Transliteration	Consonant
Heh	<u>h</u>ello	*h*	ܗ
Qop	<u>q</u>uilt	*q*	ܩ
Sade	(guttural <u>s</u>)	<u>s</u>	ܨ

Read

A.

ܗ ܗ ܗ ، ܗ̇ ܗ̇ ܗ̇ ، ܗ ܗ ܗ ، ܗ̈ ܗ̈ ܗ̈ ، ܗ ܗ ܗ .1

ܗܘ̇ܐ، ، ܗܘ ܗܘ ܗܘ ، ܗܘ ܗܘ ܗܘ ، ܗܐ ܗܐ ܗܐ

ܗܘܿܢ، ܗܘܿܕ̈ܐ، ܗܘܿܬ، ، ܗܝ، ܐܡܿܗ، ܐܗܘܿܬ؟

ܩ ܩ ܩ ، ܩ̇ ܩ̇ ܩ̇ ، ܩ ܩ ܩ ، ܩ̈ ܩ̈ ܩ̈ ، ܩ ܩ ܩ .2

ܩܘܿܬ، ، ܩܘ ܩܘ ܩܘ ، ܩܒ ܩܒ ܩܒ ، ܡܠܟܘ̈ܬܐ، ܩܠܡܘ̈ܬܐ،

ܩܠܘ̈ܠܐ، ܩܕ̈ܝܫܐ، ܚܕܘ̈ܬܐ، ܪܘܚܐ، ܗܡܙܡܘܬܐ

ܨ ܨ ܨ ، ܨ̈ ܨ̈ ܨ̈ ، ܨ̇ ܨ̇ ܨ̇ ، ܨ̣ ܨ̣ ܨ̣ ، ܨܘ̇ ܨܘ̇ ܨܘ̇ .3

، ܨܘ̇ ܨܘ̇ ܨܘ̇ ، ܨܒ ܨܒ ܨܒ ، ܨܠܘܿܬܐ، ܨܦ̈ܐ، ܨܘ̇ܡܐ، ܩܨܨ

B.

1. ܒܩܒܩܬܐ، ܩܕܡܬܐ، ܩܝܛܐ، ܩܛܘ، ܩܝܛܐ، ܒܩܒܩܬܐ
2. ܐܠܗܐ، ܗܘܢܐ، ܘܪܩܐ، ܦܘܩܐ، ܗܘܢܐ، ܐܠܗܐ، ܘܪܩܐ
3. ܣܗܪܐ، ܒܗܪܐ، ܟܗܢܐ، ܒܗܪܐ، ܣܗܪܐ
4. ܩܛܘ، ܩܝܛܐ، ܟܘܪܣܝܐ، ܩܛܘ، ܩܝܛܐ، ܬܡܗܐ
5. ܩܪܝܪܐ، ܒܗܪܐ، ܨܘܡܐ، ܩܛܘ، ܨܦܝܐ، ܩܠܘܠܐ، ܩܨܪܐ، ܦܘܩܐ
6. ܦܩܐ، ܗܘܢܢܐ، ܟܘܪܣܝܐ، ܣܬܘܐ، ܩܨܪܐ، ܫܩܘܠ، ܘܪܩܐ

Remember

Meaning	Sound	Word	Meaning	Sound	Word
nose	*poqa*	ܦܘܩܐ	God	*Alaha*	ܐܠܗܐ
Lent	*s̱awma*	ܨܘܡܐ	bubble	*baqbaqta*	ܒܩܒܩܬܐ
tomorrow	*s̱apra*	ܨܦܪܐ	light	*behra*	ܒܗܪܐ
pure	*s̱ipya*	ܨܦܝܐ	beard	*daqna*	ܕܩܢܐ
summer	*qayṯa*	ܩܝܛܐ	come	*hayyu*	ܗܝܘ
pen	*qalama*	ܩܠܡܐ	mind	*hona*	ܗܘܢܐ
quick	*qalula*	ܩܠܘܠܐ	smart	*honana*	ܗܘܢܢܐ
palace	*qas̱ra*	ܩܨܪܐ	paper	*waraqa*	ܘܪܩܐ
cold	*qaryra*	ܩܪܝܪܐ	priest	*kahna*	ܟܗܢܐ
cat	*qaṯu*	ܩܛܘ	chair	*kursya*	ܟܘܪܣܝܐ
morning	*qadamta*	ܩܕܡܬܐ	river	*nahra*	ܢܗܪܐ
market	*shuqa*	ܫܘܩܐ	moon	*sehra*	ܣܗܪܐ
take	*shqol*	ܫܩܘܠ	winter	*sitwa*	ܣܬܘܐ
why?	*ta maha*	ܬܡܗܐ	red	*smoqa*	ܣܡܘܩܐ
			frog	*piqa*	ܦܩܐ

Exercises

A.

Translate the following Chaldean words into English.

B.

Translate the following English words into Chaldean.

1. God, cross, priest
2. frog, cat, grasshopper
3. morning, dawn, light
4. moon, cold, devil

5. chair, bag, paper
6. nose, foot, beard
7. coffee, vegetables, bubble
8. summer, mind, illness

Unit 2 Review

Match each word to its translation:

God	ܢܰܗܪܳܐ
chair	ܬܰܘܪܳܐ
sea	ܙܰܩܬܳܐ
pure	ܚܘܰܕܗܳܢܳܐ
cat	ܒܰܩܪܳܐ
priest	ܥܰܘܡܳܐ
brown	ܡܰܝܳܐ
market	ܗܘܳܡܳܐ
water	ܗܘܡܰܕܢܳܐ
horse	ܚܰܘܢܳܐ
iron	ܬܰܪܒܳܐ
bird	ܝܰܒܣܳܐ
outside	ܠܰܘܩܳܠ
cheese	ܩܬܘܝܠܳܐ
red	ܗܡܚܘܡܳܐ
night	ܢܰܘܩܳܐ
dove	ܝܰܝܠܳܐ
hair	ܕܰܣܢܳܐ
beard	ܗܰܐܘܳܐ
winter	ܬܰܠܡܳܐ
pen	ܙܰܝܠܳܐ
tree	ܚܘܳܗܳܐ

21

Chapter 7

The last two letters of the alphabet to be introduced are Heth and *'e*. Like *Simkath* and *Sade*, the guttural pronunciation is what differentiates Heth from *He* and *'e* from *Alap*. Note that Heth can have two possible pronunciations, depending on the word.

Recognize

Name	As in...	Transliteration	Consonant
Heth	(guttural h) or like the *kh* sound in Bach	*h or kh*	ܚ
'e	(guttural sound)	ʻ	ܥ

Read

A.

1. ܚܲ ܚܲ ܚܲ ، ܚܵ ܚܵ ܚܵ ، ܚܹ ܚܹ ܚܹ ، ܚܸ ܚܸ ܚܸ ،
ܚܘܿ ܚܘܿ ܚܘܿ ، ܚܘܼ ܚܘܼ ܚܘܼ ، ܚܝܼ ܚܝܼ ܚܝܼ ، ܚܘܼܕܵܐ،
ܕܚܠܵܐ، ܚܲܕ̈ܕܹܐ، ܚܠܘܼܢܵܐ، ܚܡܵܫܹܐ
2. ܥܲ ܥܲ ܥܲ ، ܥܵ ܥܵ ܥܵ ، ܥܹ ܥܹ ܥܹ ، ܥܸ ܥܸ ܥܸ ،
ܥܼ ܥܼ ܥܼ ، ܥܘܿ ܥܘܿ ܥܘܿ ، ܥܘܼ ܥܘܼ ܥܘܼ ، ܥܝܼ ܥܝܼ ܥܝܼ ،
ܥܲܠܡܵܐ، ܥܝܼܠܵܢܵܐ، ܥܘܼܡܩܵܐ، ܥܲܡܘܼܡܵܐ

B.

1. ܐܘܼܪܚܵܐ، ܐܸܣܦܵܢܵܐ، ܥܲܘܠܵܐ، ܡܲܪܥܵܐ، ܚܠܘܼܢܵܐ، ܥܘܼܡܩܵܐ، ܐܘܼܪܚܵܐ
2. ܠܲܚܡܵܐ، ܚܘܼܠܡܵܐ، ܥܲܠܡܵܐ، ܕܚܡܝܵܐ، ܠܲܚܡܵܐ، ܥܲܠܡܵܐ
3. ܥܒܝܼܕܵܐ ܫܹܝܛܵܐ، ܥܡܘܼܢܵܐ، ܣܲܗܕܘܼܬܵܐ، ܒܹܥܬܵܐ، ܡܹܠܚܵܐ، ܥܲܡܡܵܐ
4. ܥܹܕܵܢܵܐ، ܥܝܼܠܵܢܵܐ، ܥܢܵܢܵܐ، ܥܢܵܢܵܐ، ܥܩܘܼܥ، ܥܹܕܵܢܵܐ، ܥܝܼܠܵܢܵܐ
5. ܚܘܼܪܙܵܐ، ܚܘܼܪܵܐ، ܚܘܼܕܪܵܐ، ܚܛܵܐ، ܚܡܸܫ ܚܲܡܫܥܵܐ، ܚܘܼܕܪܵܐ
6. ܕܪܵܥܵܐ، ܚܲܕ̈ܕܹܐ، ܚܡܸܫ، ܥܘܼܡܩܵܐ، ܐܸܣܦܵܢܵܐ، ܡܹܠܚܵܐ

Remember

Meaning	Sound	Word	Meaning	Sound	Word
door	tar'a	ܬܵܪܥܵܐ	road	'urkha	ܐܘܼܪܚܵܐ
bread	lakhma	ܠܲܚܡܵܐ	brother	akhona	ܐܲܚܘܿܢܵܐ
salt	milkha	ܡܸܠܚܵܐ	egg	be'ta	ܒܸܥܬ݂ܵܐ
stew	maraqa	ܡܵܪܲܩܵܐ	arm	dra'a	ܕܪܵܥܵܐ
time	'iddana	ܥܸܕܵܢܵܐ	dearest	habbaba	ܚܲܒܵܒ݂ܵܐ
evil	'awla	ܥܵܘܠܵܐ	apple	khabusha	ܚܲܒ݂ܘܼܫܵܐ
deep	'umqa	ܥܘܼܡܩܵܐ	love	hubba	ܚܘܼܒܵܐ
eye	'ayna	ܥܲܝܢܵܐ	dream	khulma	ܚܸܠܡܵܐ
high	'ilya	ܥܸܠܵܝܵܐ	pig	khzura	ܚܙܘܼܪܵܐ
world	'alma	ܥܵܠܡܵܐ	wheat	khitte	ܚܸܛܹܐ
with	'immid	ܥܲܡܸܕ	life	khaye	ܚܲܝܹܐ
loveliest	shamama	ܫܲܡܵܡܵܐ	sweet	haluya	ܚܲܠܘܼܝܵܐ
watermelon	shamziyya	ܫܲܡܙܝܼܵܐ	bathroom	hammam	ܚܲܡܵܡ
pretty	shappyra	ܫܲܦܝܼܪܵܐ	Jesus	Ysho'	ܝܼܫܘܿܥ
door	tar'a	ܬܵܪܥܵܐ	mercy	rahme	ܪܲܚܡܹܐ

23

Exercises

A.

Translate the following Chaldean words into English.

B.

Translate the following English words into Chaldean.

1. road, bathroom, pig
2. with, apple, watermelon
3. sweet, pretty, high
4. wheat, salt, gravy

5. evil, mercy, life
6. Jesus, love, world
7. arm, eye, brother
8. deep, dream, loveliest

Chapter 8

Chapter 8 introduces the modifiable letters. Six letters in the Chaldean alphabet can be modified to form new consonant sounds: *Weth, Ghamal, Dhalath, Khap, Phe* and *Thaw*. A dot or semi-circle is placed below the letter to signify the change.

Recognize

Name	As in…	Transliteration	Letter
Weth	<u>w</u>ow	w	ܒ
Ghamal	(softened g)	gh	ܓ
Dhalath	<u>the</u>	dh	ܕ
Khap	Ba<u>ch</u>	kh	ܟ
Phe	<u>ph</u>one or <u>w</u>ow	ph or w	ܦ
Thaw	<u>th</u>ick	th	ܬ

Read

A.

1. ܒܹ ، ܒܿ ، ܒܲ ، ܒܵ ، ܒܸ ، ܒܹ ، ܒܘ ، ܒܼ

2. ܓ ، ܓܿ ، ܓܲ ، ܓܹ ، ܓ ، ܓܹ ، ܓܘ ، ܓܼ

3. ܕ ، ܕܿ ، ܕܲ ، ܕܹ ، ܕ ، ܕܹ ، ܕܘ ، ܕܼ

4. ܟ ، ܟܿ ، ܟܲ ، ܟ ، ܟ ، ܟ ، ܟܘ ، ܟܼ

5. ܦ ، ܦܿ ، ܦܲ ، ܦ ، ܦ ، ܦ ، ܦܘ ، ܦܼ

6. ܬ ، ܬܿ ، ܬ ، ܬ ، ܬ ، ܬ ، ܬܘ ، ܬܼ

B.

1. ܐܒܗ̈ܐ، ܓܒܪܐ، ܓܢܒܐ، ܕܒܫܐ، ܙܒܢܐ، ܟܘܟܒܐ
2. ܦܓܪܐ، ܫܓܝܫܐ، ܨܠܝܒܐ، ܛܒܐ
3. ܓܕܕܐ، ܢܩܝܕܐ، ܥܒܕܐ، ܩܕܝܠܐ، ܪܩܕܐ
4. ܒܪܝܟܐ، ܝܪܝܟܐ، ܟܘܟܒܐ، ܡܠܐܟܐ، ܢܟܦܬܐ
5. ܣܦܘܪܐ، ܦܗܡܐ، ܩܦܝܠܐ، ܬܘܬܐ
6. ܒܝܬܐ، ܟܬܒܐ ܩܕܝܫܐ، ܨܠܘܬܐ

Remember

Meaning	Sound	Word	Meaning	Sound	Word
chaste	*nakhopta*	ܢܟܦܬܐ	parents	*awahi*	ܐܒܗ̈ܐ
thin	*nqydha*	ܢܩܝܕܐ	house	*betha*	ܒܝܬܐ
traveling	*saphori*	ܣܦܘܪܐ	blessed	*brykha*	ܒܪܝܟܐ
act	*'wadha*	ܥܒܕܐ	man; husband	*gawara*	ܓܒܪܐ
body	*paghra*	ܦܓܪܐ	thief	*ganawa*	ܓܢܒܐ
understanding	*ph-hama*	ܦܗܡܐ	string	*gdhadha*	ܓܕܕܐ
prayer	*s̲lotha*	ܨܠܘܬܐ	honey	*diwsha*	ܕܒܫܐ
cross	*s̲lywa*	ܨܠܝܒܐ	time	*zawna*	ܙܒܢܐ
key	*qdhyla*	ܩܕܝܠܐ	good	*t̲awa*	ܛܒܐ
locked	*qphyla*	ܩܦܝܠܐ	long	*yarykha*	ܝܪܝܟܐ
dancing	*rqadha*	ܪܩܕܐ	star	*kawkhwa*	ܟܘܟܒܐ
troubled	*shghysha*	ܫܓܝܫܐ	Bible	*kthawa qaddysha*	ܟܬܒܐ ܩܕܝܫܐ
fig	*tutha*	ܬܘܬܐ	angel	*malakha*	ܡܠܐܟܐ

Exercises

A.

Translate the following Chaldean words into English.

5. ܟܬܒܐ، ܦܠܓܐ، ܦܘܩܕܐ
6. ܟܘܝܐ، ܚܡܬܐ، ܬܘܝܬܐ، ܟܬܐ
7. ܚܡܬܐ، ܬܘܝܬܐ، ܕܬܝܐ
8. ܪܩܕܐ، ܚܘܚܬܐ، ܥܒܬܐ

1. ܗܘܗܐ، ܢܚܘܩܐ، ܩܘܩܡܐ
2. ܡܠܪܚܐ، ܟܬܝܐ، ܘܚܢܐ
3. ܢܣܒܝܐ، ܬܕܒܚܐ، ܝܟܒܬܐ
4. ܝܟܦܗܐ، ܢܬܒܚܐ، ܬܘܝܟܐ

B.

Translate the following English words into Chaldean

1. parents, man, thief
2. Bible, cross, prayer
3. star, time, angel
4. shy, long, troubled

5. honey, fig, body, string
6. good, act, thin
7. dancing, locked, house
8. key, understanding, traveling

Chapter 9

A second modification is possible for the letters *Beth, Gamal, Teth* and *Kap* with the addition of a half circle placed under the letter. Two symbols introduced here are the single slash (*mbaṯlana*) placed over a letter to indicate that the letter is silent, as well as the plural sign called *syame*.

Recognize

Name	As in...	Transliteration	Letter
Veth	<u>v</u>ery	v	ܒ݂
Jamal	<u>j</u>azz	j	ܓ݂
Dthe	(guttural <u>t</u>)	dth	ܛ݂
Chap	<u>ch</u>op	ch	ܟ݂

Name	Meaning	Symbol
Mbaṯlana	silent	�
Syame	plural	�

Read

A.

ܒ݁ , ܒ݂ , ܒܹ , ܒ݂ , ܒܹ݁ , ܒ݂ܹ , ܒܹ݁ , ܒ݂ܹ .1

ܓ݂ , ܓ݂ , ܓ݂ , ܓ݂ , ܓ݂ܹ , ܓ݂ܹ , ܓ݂ܹ , ܓ݂ܹ .2

ܛ݂ , ܛ݂ , ܛ݂ , ܛ݂ , ܛ݂ܹ , ܛ݂ܹ , ܛ݂ܹ , ܛ݂ܹ .3

ܟ݂ , ܟ݂ , ܟ݂ , ܟ݂ , ܟ݂ܹ , ܟ݂ܹ , ܟ݂ܹ , ܟ݂ܹ .4

B.

1. ܟ̰ܲܡܟ̰ܵܐ، ܟܲܪܣܵܐ، ܟܲܦܵܐ، ܟ̰ܲܝ، ܩܲܪܓ̰ܵܠܵܐ، ܟ̰ܘܼܡܝܼܢܕܝܼ
2. ܡܲܡܠܠܵܐ، ܐܪܵܙܵܐ، ܡܕܝܼܢ݇ܬܵܐ، ܐܲܓܵܪܵܐ، ܐ݈ܢܵܫܵܐ، ܐܪܵܙܵܐ
3. ܨ̰ܸܒܝܘܿܢܵܐ، ܓ̰ܘܼܠܠܹܐ، ܓ̰ܘܼܒܝܹܐ، ܦܲܠܓܘܼ
4. ܩܲܪܢܵܐ، ܫܲܢ݇ܬܵܐ، ܓܲܢܒܵܪܵܐ، ܡܕܝܼܢ݇ܬܵܐ، ܐܲܓܵܪܵܐ، ܐ݈ܢܵܫܵܐ
5. ܐ݈ܢܵܫܵܐ ܕܡܕܝܼܢ݇ܬܵܐ، ܩܲܪܓ̰ܵܠܵܐ ܓܲܢܒܵܪܵܐ، ܟ̰ܲܢܓܲܠ ܘܟ̰ܲܡܟ̰ܵܐ

Remember

Meaning	Sound	Word	Meaning	Sound	Word
nothing	*chumindy*	ܟ̰ܘܼܡܝܼܢܕܝܼ	roof	*gari*	ܐܲܓܵܪܵܐ
big spoon	*chamcha*	ܟ̰ܲܡܟ̰ܵܐ	person	*nasha*	ܐ݈ܢܵܫܵܐ
belly	*kasa*	ܟܲܪܣܵܐ	mass	*'raza*	ܐܪܵܙܵܐ
speech	*mamla*	ܡܲܡܠܠܵܐ	clothes	*julli*	ܓ̰ܘܼܠܠܹܐ
city	*mdhyta*	ܡܕܝܼܢ݇ܬܵܐ	group	*jwyni*	ܓ̰ܘܼܒܝܹܐ
will	*'ijbona*	ܨ̰ܸܒܝܘܿܢܵܐ	mighty	*gabbara*	ܓܲܢܒܵܪܵܐ
mid-Lent	*palu*	ܦܲܠܓܘܼ	one	*kha*	ܚܲܕ
piece	*parcha*	ܦܲܪܟ̰ܵܐ	under	*kho*	ܬܚܘܿܬ
turtle	*qarjala*	ܩܲܪܓ̰ܵܠܵܐ	fork	*changal*	ܟ̰ܲܢܓܲܠ
horn	*qarna*	ܩܲܪܢܵܐ	handful	*kaffa*	ܟܲܦܵܐ
year	*shata*	ܫܲܢ݇ܬܵܐ	tea	*chay*	ܟ̰ܲܝ

Exercises

A.

Translate the following Chaldean words into English.

ܠܘܟܠܝ، ܚܘܡܝܝܒ، ܒܝܟܕܝ .1

ܝܢܬܝ، ܥܢܬܐ، ܝܢܝܠ .2

ܚܡܚܝ، ܚܘܝ، ܝܒ .3

ܒܕܝܠܝ، ܡܡܠܠܝ، ܦܕܝ .4

ܝܕܘܝ، ܝܝܚܡܢܝ، ܒܕܢܝ .5

ܣܘܗ، ܒܝܝ، ܚܕܗܝ، ܦܠܟܗ .6

ܠܘܒܝܝ، ܡܕܒܬܡܐ، ܠܒܬܕܝ .7

B.

Translate the following English words into Chaldean.

1. clothes, person, piece
2. one, handful, group
3. serving spoon, tea
4. nothing, fork, year

5. mid-Lent, Mass, belly
6. city, horn, mighty
7. under, turtle, speech

Unit 3 Review

Match each word to its translation:

path	ܐܪܘܿܚܵܐ
dancing	ܚܸܠܵܢ
salt	ܕܸܒܥܵܐ
honey	ܕܸܡܕܵܐ
fork	ܡܵܪܝܼܡܸܐ
troubled	ܙܲܠܵܐ
brother	ܐܲܚܘܿܢܵܐ
watermelon	ܚܵܒܘܿܣܵܐ
city	ܡܸܢܕܝܼ
will	ܝܵܠܝܼܕܵܐ
house	ܒܲܝܬܵܐ
egg	ܬܲܪܵܐ
eye	ܐܲܝܢܵܐ
apple	ܚܘܿܡܝܼܒ
horn	ܩܲܕܢܵܐ
person	ܫܲܚܘܿܐܵܐ
nothing	ܚܲܒܵܐ
love	ܚܘܿܒܘܿܐ
angel	ܡܲܠܲܐܟ݂ܵܐ
Mass	ܩܘܿܪܵܐ
prayer	ܨܲܠܘܿܬܵܐ
year	ܫܸܢܬܵܐ

Chapter 10
Greetings and Basic Phrases

Language   لٕغْذَ

While there are many elements of the Chaldean language that are quite simple, other things need some explanation. For example, saying "hello" isn't as easy as it is in English. The idiom (that is, the way the language works) in Chaldean is that the way to say "hello" to someone is to use the phrase "peace be with you." That is the most basic greeting.

While it's totally acceptable to simply greet someone in Chaldean just by saying *Shlama* ("Peace!"), it is more proper to add "with you." But this makes things a little more complicated, because there are three ways to say "you" in Chaldean – one for addressing a man, one for addressing a woman, and one for addressing a group of people. You do it by using these "endings":

you (m)	*ukh*	ڡٛٯ
you (f)	*akh*	ڡٛ
you (pl)	*okhun*	ٯٮحٯ

So piecing together what we know, we take the word for "peace" (*shlama*), then the word for "upon" ('*ill*), and add whichever ending above matches the person or people you're addressing:

Peace be upon you (m)	*Shlama illukh*	ܫܠܵܡܵ ܥܸܠܠܘܟ
Peace be upon you (f)	*Shlama illakh*	ܫܠܵܡܵ ܥܸܠܠܝ
Peace be upon you (pl)	*Shlama illokhun*	ܫܠܵܡܵ ܥܸܠܠܟܘܢ

All this just to say hello! But the usual response is pretty simple, and doesn't change no matter who you say it to:

In peace & blessings	*b-shayna w-btawatha*	ܒܫܲܝܢܵ ܘܒܬܲܘܵܬܼܵ

Or you could respond with the appropriate version of *shlama illukh*, as in the conversation below.

Saying "welcome" works in the same way. The English word "welcome" is a combination of two words: "well come!" Again, Chaldean uses the concept of peace in its greetings. Instead of saying that the person who arrived has come "well," we say he has come "in peace." And just like above, depending on whom you're talking to, the endings of the word will change:

Welcome (m)	*b-shayna thelukh*	ܒܫܝܢܐ ܬܹܠܘܟ݂
Welcome (f)	*b-shayna thelakh*	ܒܫܝܢܐ ܬܹܠܵܟ݂
Welcome (pl)	*b-shayna thelokhun*	ܒܫܝܢܐ ܬܹܠܵܟ݂ܘܢ

The proper response to this is literally to say "Peace yourself!" But it really means "Peace to you too!" Again, you'd use one of the same three endings at the end of the word "self:"

Peace to you too (m)	*b-shayna gyanukh*	ܒܫܝܢܐ ܓܝܵܢܘܟ݂
Peace to you too (f)	*b-shayna gyanakh*	ܒܫܝܢܐ ܓܝܵܢܵܟ݂
Peace to you too (pl)	*bshayna gyanokhun*	ܒܫܝܢܐ ܓܝܵܢܵܟ݂ܘܢ

So far we see that Chaldean is a very peace-full language. But it's also a very religious language. The closest equivalent to saying "please" is to say "God forgive you!"

Please (m)	*Alaha Shawiq-lukh*	ܐܲܠܵܗܵܐ ܫܵܒܹܩ ܠܘܟ݂
Please (f)	*Alaha Shawiq-lakh*	ܐܲܠܵܗܵܐ ܫܵܒܹܩ ܠܵܟ݂
Please (pl)	*Alaha Shawiq-lokhun*	ܐܲܠܵܗܵܐ ܫܵܒܹܩ ܠܵܟ݂ܘܢ

Again, it's the same endings that are used in all of these different phrases.

Saying "thank you" works similarly, and is literally translated "may your soul be pleased:"

Thank you (m)	*basma gyanukh*	ܬܘܤܡܐ ܠܓܢܘܟ
Thank you (f)	*basma gyanakh*	ܬܘܤܡܐ ܠܓܢܟܝ
Thank you (pl)	*basma gyanokhun*	ܬܘܤܡܐ ܠܓܢܘܟܘܢ

If you want to say "goodbye," two different phrases can work. The first is to say "God be with you:"

God be with you (m)	*Alaha immukh*	ܐܠܗܐ ܥܡܘܟ
God be with you (f)	*Alaha immakh*	ܐܠܗܐ ܥܡܟܝ
God be with you (pl)	*Alaha immokhun*	ܐܠܗܐ ܥܡܘܟܘܢ

The second way to say goodbye is to say "remain in peace." Here the "endings" you learned above won't work, and the word for "remain" changes slightly, depending on if you're talking to one or to many people. Masculine and feminine don't make a difference here:

Remain in peace (s)	*posh bi-shlama*	ܦܘܫ ܒܫܠܡܐ
Remain in peace (pl)	*pushu bi-shlama*	ܦܘܫܘ ܒܫܠܡܐ

Chapter 10

Conversation ܡܫܥܝܬܐ

The Conversations given in each chapter are meant to be challenging. Using the Grammar and Vocabulary of this chapter and what you know from earlier chapters, try to understand as much as you can.

Mariam	Hello, David.	ܫܠܡܐ ܥܠܘܟ، ܕܘܝܕ.	ܡܪܝܡ
David	Hello, Mariam.	ܫܠܡܐ ܥܠܟܝ، ܡܪܝܡ.	ܕܘܝܕ
Mariam	How are you?	ܕܝܟ ܐܝܘܬ؟	ܡܪܝܡ
David	Fine. How are you?	ܛܒܐ. ܕܝܟ ܐܝܘܬܝ ܐܢܬܝ؟	ܕܘܝܕ
Mariam	Fine. This is my friend Katherine.	ܛܒܐ. ܐܗܝ ܝܠܗ ܚܒܪܬܝ ܟܬܪܝܢܐ.	ܡܪܝܡ
David	Welcome, Katherine.	ܒܫܝܢܐ ܐܬܝܬܝ، ܟܬܪܝܢܐ.	ܕܘܝܕ
Katie	Welcome to you, David.	ܒܫܝܢܐ ܠܓܢܘܟ، ܕܘܝܕ.	ܟܬܪܝܢܐ
David	What is your father's name?	ܡܘܝܠܗ ܫܡܐ ܕܒܒܟܝ؟	ܕܘܝܕ
Katie	My father's name is Joseph Nagara.	ܫܡܐ ܕܒܒܝ ܝܠܗ ܝܘܣܦ ܕܒܝ ܢܓܪܐ.	ܟܬܪܝܢܐ
David	Yes, I know him well. Greet him for me, please.	ܐܝܢ، ܟܝܕܥܢ ܠܗ ܛܒܐ. ܡܫܐܠ ܠܝ ܒܫܠܡܗ، ܐܠܗܐ ܥܡܡ ܠܝ.	ܕܘܝܕ
Katie	I'm sure he greets you as well. Thank you.	ܟܡܫܐܠ ܥܠܘܟ ܒܗܕܟܐ. ܒܣܝܡܐ ܠܓܢܘܟ.	ܟܬܪܝܢܐ
Mariam	God with you, David. Goodbye.	ܐܠܗܐ ܥܡܘܟ، ܕܘܝܕ. ܦܘܫ ܒܫܠܡܐ.	ܡܪܝܡ
David	Goodbye.	ܦܘܫܘ ܒܫܠܡܐ.	ܕܘܝܕ

Vocabulary ܡܹܠܬܵܐ

Meaning	Sound	Word	Meaning	Sound	Word
upon	ill	ܥܲܠ	this	adhy	ܐܵܗܵܕܝ
with	imm	ܥܲܡ	yes	e	ܐܹ
remain	posh	ܦܘܿܫ	self/soul	gyana	ܓܝܵܢܵܐ
well	randa	ܪܵܢܕܵܐ	friend	khawra	ܚܲܒܪܵܐ
forgive	shaweq	ܫܒܘܿܩ	good	ṭawta	ܛܵܒܘܼܬ݂ܵܐ
peace	shayna	ܫܲܝܢܵܐ	behalf	kepha	ܟܹܐܦ݂ܵܐ
name	shimma	ܫܸܡܵܐ	carpenter	nagara	ܢܲܓܵܪܵܐ

Here are the Idioms (phrases unique to a language) that you learned this chapter:

Idiomatically	Literally	Sound	Phrase
hello	peace upon you	shlama illukh	ܫܠܵܡܵܐ ܥܲܠܘܼܟ݂
hello (response)	in peace and blessings	bshayna w-bṭawatha	ܒܫܲܝܢܵܐ ܘܬܛܵܒܵܬ݂ܵܐ
welcome	you have come in peace	bshayna thelukh	ܒܫܲܝܢܵܐ ܐܵܬ݂ܹܠܘܼܟ݂
welcome (response)	peace yourself	bshayna gyanukh	ܒܫܲܝܢܵܐ ܓܝܵܢܘܼܟ݂
please	God forgive you	Alaha shawiq lukh	ܐܲܠܵܗܵܐ ܫܒܘܿܩ ܠܘܼܟ݂
thank you	may your soul be pleased	basma gyanukh	ܒܲܣܡܵܐ ܓܝܵܢܘܼܟ݂
goodbye	God be with you	Alaha immukh	ܐܲܠܵܗܵܐ ܥܲܡܘܼܟ݂
goodbye	remain in peace	posh bishlama	ܦܘܿܫ ܒܸܫܠܵܡܵܐ

Remember that some of the "endings" of the words change depending on whom you're speaking to:

you (pl) ܘܿܟ݂ܘܿܢ	you (f) ܐܲܟ݂ܝ	you (m) ܘܼܟ݂

36

Exercise ܗܿܢܹܐ

1. Write in Chaldean how you would say "Hello" to the following:
   A. Your brother.
   B. Your sister.
   C. Your parents.

2. How would you say "Welcome" to each of the above?

3. How would you tell each of the above "God be with you"?

4. How would you tell each of the above "Thank you"?

5. Read through the conversation above. Explain the Chaldean words and phrases you understand, and circle the ones you don't understand yet.

Chaldean Culture ܟܲܠܕܵܝܘܼܬܵܐ

When meeting someone new, it is polite to shake hands while introducing yourself. However, when greeting a friend or family member, Chaldeans traditionally embrace and give a slight kiss on each cheek. When parting, the same ritual may be repeated.

Chapter 11
Home and Family
Possessive Pronouns; Prepositions

Possessive Pronouns in English are words that show ownership, like "my" in the phrase "my house" and "your" as in "your boat." In Chaldean, instead of using independent words, special "endings" are attached to the end of the noun that we are talking about. In the previous chapter, we saw this phrase:

ܢܸܦܫܘܿܟ ܒܣܝܼܡܬܸ

This literally means "your soul be pleased." So the second word is a combination of the word for "soul" and the ending that indicates "your:"

ܢܸܦܫܘܿܟ = ܘܿܟ + ܢܸܦܫ

Here is the full set of endings:

Meaning	Sound	Ending
my	y	ـܝ
your (m)	ukh	ܘܿܟ
your (f)	akh	ܟ
his	eh	ܗ
her	ah	ܗ
our	an	ܢ
your (pl)	okhun	ܘܿܟ݂ܘܢ
their	ay	ܠܲܝܗ

You can combine these endings with any noun to indicate possession. For example:

Meaning	Sound	Word
my name	shimmy	ܫܸܡܝ
your (m) name	shimmukh	ܫܸܡܘܼܟ݂
your (f) name	shimmakh	ܫܸܡܵܟ݂
his name	shimmeh	ܫܸܡܹܗ
her name	shimmah	ܫܸܡܵܗ̇
our name	shimman	ܫܸܡܲܢ
your (pl) name	shimmokhun	ܫܸܡܵܘܟ݂ܘܿܢ
their name	shimmay	ܫܸܡܲܝܗܝ

These same endings are used with other kinds of words as well, so make sure to learn them until they become second nature. One of the places these endings are used is with prepositions like "from" or "with." You remember the phrase *shlama illukh* from last chapter – the second word is an example of this:

Meaning	Sound	Word
upon me	illy	ܥܠܝ
upon you (m)	illukh	ܥܠܘܼܟ݂
upon you (f)	illakh	ܥܠܵܟ݂
upon him	illeh	ܥܠܹܗ
upon her	illah	ܥܠܵܗ̇
upon us	illan	ܥܠܲܢ
upon you (pl)	illokhun	ܥܠܵܘܟ݂ܘܿܢ
upon them	illay	ܥܠܲܝܗܝ

39

These endings work with any of the "separable" prepositions:

Meaning	Sound	Word
in me, in you...	bgawy, bgawukh...	...ܓܲܘܘܼܟ݂، ܓܲܘܝ
after me, after you...	bathry, bathrukh...	...ܒܵܬ݂ܪܘܼܟ݂، ܒܵܬ݂ܪܝ
for me, for you...	ṭaly, ṭalukh...	...ܛܲܠܘܼܟ݂، ܛܲܠܝ
from me, from you...	minny, minnukh...	...ܡܸܢܘܼܟ݂، ܡܸܢܝ
upon me, upon you...	illy, illukh...	...ܐܸܠܘܼܟ݂، ܐܸܠܝ
with me, with you...	immy, immukh...	...ܥܸܡܘܼܟ݂، ܥܸܡܝ

Other prepositions, called "inseparable," are attached to the beginning of nouns. There are six of them:

Meaning	Sound	Preposition
in	b	ܒ
of	d	ܕ
and	w	ܘ
to/for	l	ܠ
like	kh	ܟ݂
from	m	ܡ

Here they are combined with some nouns so you can see how they work:

Meaning	Sound	Preposition
in the book	bi-kthawa	ܒܟ݂ܵܬ݂ܵܒ݂ܵ
of the king	d-malka	ܕܡܲܠܟܵ
and the mountain	w-ṭura	ܘܛܘܼܪܵ
to/for the man	l-gawra	ܠܓܲܒ݂ܪܵ
like a bear	kh-dibba	ܟ݂ܕܸܒܵ
from the house	m-betha	ܡܒܲܝܬ݂ܵ

40

If you're wondering why some of the examples above have the *i* vowel under the preposition, it's because the letter next to it doesn't have any vowel at all, and the whole word would be impossible to pronounce without it.

Conversation ܡܫܚܕܬܐ

Mariam	Welcome, David.	ܒܫܝܢܐ ܐܬܠܘܟ، ܕܘܝܕ.	ܡܪܝܡ
David	Thank you, Mariam.	ܒܫܝܢܐ ܠܓܢܘܟܝ، ܡܪܝܡ.	ܕܘܝܕ
Mariam	These are my relatives inside the house.	ܐܗܢܝ ܝܠܗܘܢ ܩܪܝܒܘܝ ܓܘ ܒܝܬܐ.	ܡܪܝܡ
David	Who is in the den?	ܡܢܝ ܝܠܗܘܢ ܒܕܝܘܢ؟	ܕܘܝܕ
Mariam	They are my mother and father.	ܝܡܝ ܘܒܒܝ ܝܠܗܘܢ.	ܡܪܝܡ
David	And who is in the dining room?	ܘܡܢܝ ܝܠܗܘܢ ܒܐܘܕܐ ܕܐܟܠܐ؟	ܕܘܝܕ
Mariam	Those are my grandmother and aunt, and with them my sister and her youngest daughter.	ܐܗܢܝ ܝܠܗܘܢ ܢܢܝ ܘܚܠܬܝ، ܘܥܡܝܗܘܢ ܚܬܝ ܘܒܪܬܗ ܙܥܘܪܬܐ.	ܡܪܝܡ
David	And this chair in the middle of the sitting room, whose is it?	ܘܐܗܐ ܟܘܪܣܝܐ ܒܦܠܓܐ ܕܐܘܕܐ ܕܝܬܒܐ، ܕܡܢܝ ܝܠܗ؟	ܕܘܝܕ
Mariam	That chair is my grandfather's, the great father of our family.	ܐܗܘ ܟܘܪܣܝܐ ܝܠܗ ܕܣܒܝ، ܒܒܐ ܪܒܐ ܕܒܝܬܘܬܢ.	ܡܪܝܡ
David	The grandfather and grandmother are the king and queen of the family.	ܣܒܐ ܘܣܒܬܐ ܝܠܗܘܢ ܡܠܟܐ ܘܡܠܟܬܐ ܕܒܝܬܘܬܐ.	ܕܘܝܕ

Vocabulary ܡܝ̈ܟܟܕ

Meaning	Sound	Word	Meaning	Sound	Word
bath room	_hammam_	ܚܡܡ	dining room	awda d-ykhala	ܐܘܕܐ ܕܝܡܚܠܐ
chair	kursya	ܟܘܪܣܝܐ	sitting room	awda d-ytawa	ܐܘܕܐ ܕܝܬܒܐ
kitchen	matbakh	ܡܛܒܟ	bedroom	awda di-dmakha	ܐܘܕܐ ܕܕܡܟܐ
table	mez	ܡܝܙ	den	y-wan	ܐܝܘܢ
relatives	nashwatha	ܢܫ̈ܘܬܐ	floor	ar'a	ܐܪܥܐ
pillo	stabytha	ܣܡܟܬܐ	blanket	batana	ܒܛܢܐ
couch	qanapa	ܩܢܦܐ	family	bethutha	ܒܝܬܘܬܐ
window	shibbak	ܫܒܟ	garden	bistana	ܒܣܬܢܐ
bed	shwytha	ܫܘܝܬܐ	closet	dulaba	ܕܘܠܒܐ

	Grandmother ܩܫܬܐ	Grandfather ܩܫܐ	
Maternal Uncle ܚܠܐ	Mother ܝܡܐ	Father ܒܒܐ	Paternal Uncle ܥܡܐ
Maternal Aunt ܚܠܬܐ	**Family Members**		Paternal Aunt ܥܡܬܐ
Sister ܚܬܐ	Wife ܒܟܬܐ	Husband ܓܒܪܐ	Brother ܐܚܘܢܐ
	Daughter ܒܪܬܐ	Son ܒܪܘܢܐ	
	Granddaughter ܢܦܩܬܐ	Grandson ܢܦܩܐ	

Cousins, nephews and nieces are described like this:

Son of my brother	Daughter of my maternal uncle
ܒܪ ܕܐܚܘܢܝ	ܒܪܬܐ ܕܚܠܝ

Exercise ܗܢܝܢܐ

1. Write the following in English:

ܗ . ܗܬܝ   ܐ . ܐܚܘܢܝ

ܘ . ܚܡܗ   ܒ . ܠܒܝܬ ܬܒܘܬܟܘܢ

ܙ . ܠܒܝܢܝ   ܓ . ܒܪ ܫܠܡܘܬܗ

ܚ . ܒܪܬܐ ܕܐܚܘܢܝ   ܕ . ܗܬܘܗܝ

2. Write the following in Chaldean:

A. From your (m) brother   E. Like your (f) nephew
B. His sister   F. Our family
C. Their mother   G. Of her grandfather
D. In my bed   H. And to my paternal uncle

3. Compose 7 short phrases in Chaldean using the material you've learned so far.

4. Read through the conversation above. Explain the Chaldean words and phrases you understand, and circle the ones you don't understand yet.

Chaldean Culture ܟܠܕܝܘܬܐ

Chaldean families are known to be quite large, with the number of cousins sometimes exceeding 100! Distant relatives may never be known, but some have found them easy to identify by asking what village in Iraq their family came from. Some discover that their grandparents, or great grandparents, even 'shared a wall' in Iraq. That literally means that the house their grandparents lived in were separated only by a wall.

Chapter 12
The Garden;
Male, Female and Plural Nouns and Adjectives

Chaldean nouns and adjectives look very similar, especially in their "endings," which indicate if they are masculine or feminine, and singular or plural.

Masculine nouns and adjectives usually end in an *a* sound, with an *Alap* at the end of the word. Feminine nouns end with a *Taw* before the final *Alap*:

Feminine Nouns			Masculine Nouns		
Meaning	Sound	Word	Meaning	Sound	Word
year	shata	ܫܲܢ݇ܬܵܐ	lion	arya	ܐܲܪܝܵܐ
mare	susta	ܣܘܼܣܬܵܐ	chair	kursya	ܟܘܼܪܣܝܵܐ
girl	brata	ܒܪܵܬܵܐ	fruit	pera	ܦܹܐܪܵܐ

There is no "neuter" in Chaldean. That means there is no "it;" grammatically speaking, everything is either "he" or "she."

You can also recognize plural nouns from their endings. Most of the time, masculine plurals only change the ending from the *a* vowel to the *i* vowel (*zqapa* to *zlama*):

Masculine Plural			Masculine Singular		
Meaning	Sound	Word	Meaning	Sound	Word
lions	aryi	ܐܲܪܝܹܐ	lion	arya	ܐܲܪܝܵܐ
kings	malki	ܡܲܠܟܹܐ	king	malka	ܡܲܠܟܵܐ
fruits	peri	ܦܹܐܪܹܐ	fruit	pera	ܦܹܐܪܵܐ

Remember from earlier in the book that the two square dots above a word (called *syame*) indicate that it is plural.

Feminine plurals can often have the same ending as masculine plurals, but there is also a special feminine plural form:

Feminine Plural			Feminine Singular		
Meaning	Sound	Word	Meaning	Sound	Word
mares	*susyatha*	ܣܘܣ̈ܝܬܐ	mare	*susta*	ܣܘܣܬܐ
sisters	*khathwatha*	ܚ̈ܬܘܬܐ	sister	*khatha*	ܚܬܐ
sins	*khtyatha*	ܚ̈ܛܝܬܐ	sin	*khtytha*	ܚܛܝܬܐ

Adjectives work in the same way. There are masculine and feminine, and singular and plural adjectives, and they generally use the exact same endings as nouns, so there's almost nothing to memorize.

Feminine	Masculine	"large"
ܪܒܬܐ	ܪܒܐ	Singular
ܪܒܐ	ܪܒܐ	Plural

Note that, like mentioned above, the feminine plural is usually the same as the masculine plural.

The way these adjectives are used is that they follow the same gender and number as the noun they modify. So if you want to say "large donkey," you have a masculine singular noun "donkey," so you would use the masculine singular form of the adjective:

Feminine	Masculine	"large donkey"
ܚܡܪܬܐ ܪܒܬܐ	ܚܡܪܐ ܪܒܐ	Singular
ܚܡܪܬܐ ܪܒܐ	ܚܡܪܐ ܪܒܐ	Plural

Notice also that, unlike in English, the adjective comes *after* the noun in the sentence. In dictionaries, adjectives are found in the masculine singular form, and it's up to you to adapt them to the feminine or plural forms.

Conversation ܡܫܥܝܬܐ

Mariam	This is the garden of our house, David.	ܐܗܝ ܐܝܠܗ ܒܘܣܬܢܐ ܕܒܝܬܢ، ܕܘܝܕ.	ܡܪܝܡ
David	It's beautiful. What is that small tree?	ܫܦܝܪܬܐ ܐܝܠܗ. ܡܢܝܠܗ ܐܗܘ ܐܝܠܢܐ ܙܥܘܪܐ؟	ܕܘܝܕ
Mariam	That is a pomegranate tree.	ܐܗܘ ܐܝܠܗ ܐܝܠܢܐ ܕܪܘܡܢܐ.	ܡܪܝܡ
David	And near it is a tree of large apples.	ܘܩܘܪܒܗ ܐܝܬ ܚܕ ܐܝܠܢܐ ܕܚܙܘܪܐ ܪܒܐ.	ܕܘܝܕ
Mariam	How many apricots are over there?	ܘܟܡܐ ܐܝܠܝ ܐܗܘܢ ܡܫܡܫܐ ܬܡܐ؟	ܡܪܝܡ
David	In front of my eyes I see twenty-five.	ܩܕܡ ܥܝܢܝ ܚܙܝܢ ܥܣܪܝܢ ܘܚܡܫܐ.	ܕܘܝܕ
Mariam	And what's on that far tree?	ܘܡܐ ܐܝܬ ܒܐܗܘ ܐܝܠܢܐ ܪܚܘܩܐ؟	ܡܪܝܡ
David	There are many sweet figs. How do these trees grow?	ܐܝܬ ܬܐܢܐ ܟܒܝܪܐ ܘܚܠܝܐ. ܕܝܟ ܪܒܝܢ ܐܢܝ ܐܝܠܢܐ؟	ܕܘܝܕ
Mariam	They grow from the work of the hand, love of the house, and the power of the soil, the sun and the rain from God.	ܪܒܝܢ ܡܢ ܥܘܒܕܐ ܕܐܝܕܐ، ܘܚܘܒܐ ܕܒܝܬܐ، ܘܚܝܠܐ ܕܐܘܦܪܐ ܘܫܡܫܐ ܘܡܛܪܐ ܡܢ ܐܠܗܐ.	ܡܪܝܡ

Vocabulary ܡܶܠܬܐ

Meaning	Sound	Word	Meaning	Sound	Word
lettuce	khass	ܚܣܐ	tree	ylana	ܐܝܠܢܐ
apricot	mishmish	ܡܫܡܫܐ	dirt	upra	ܐܘܦܪܐ
grape	inwa	ܥܢܒܐ	pomegra-nate	armona	ܪܘܡܢܐ
plum	'injasa	ܐܢܓܨܐ	eggplant	banjana	ܒܢܓܢܐ
orange	purtaqal	ܦܘܪܬܩܠ	melon	bashyla	ܒܛܝܟܐ
potato	pa_ta_ta	ܦܛܛܐ	grass	gilla	ܓܠܐ
bean	fasulya	ܦܨܘܠܝܐ	flower	warda	ܘܪܕܐ
cauli-flower	qarnaby_t	ܩܪܢܒܝܛ	manure	zibla	ܘܒܠܐ
squash	qar'a	ܩܪܥܐ	apple	khabusha	ܚܒܘܫܐ
water-melon	shamziya	ܫܡܙܝܐ	mud	_tyna	ܛܝܢܐ
fig	tena	ܬܐܢܐ	tomato	_tama_ta	ܛܡܛܐ
mulberry	tutha	ܬܘܬܐ	cucumber	khyar	ܚܝܪܐ

Remember that adjectives are given in the masculine singular, and need to be changed to feminine or plural depending on the noun they are modifying:

Meaning	Sound	Word	Meaning	Sound	Word
hungry	kpyna	ܟܦܝܢܐ	evil	bysha	ܒܝܫܐ
sick	kryha	ܟܪܝܗܐ	blessed	brykha	ܒܪܝܟܐ
deep	'amuqa	ܥܡܘܩܐ	small	z'ora	ܙܥܘܪܐ
pure	_sipya	ܨܦܝܐ	just	zaddyqa	ܙܕܝܩܐ
holy	qaddysha	ܩܕܝܫܐ	wise	_hakkyma	ܚܟܝܡܐ
large	raba	ܪܒܐ	sweet	khilya	ܚܠܝܐ

47

Meaning	Sound	Word	Meaning	Sound	Word
far	*rahuqa*	ܪܚܘܩܐ	good	*tawa*	ܛܒܐ
beautiful	*shappyra*	ܫܦܝܪܐ	many	*kabyra*	ܟܒܝܪܐ

Numbers from 1 to 10 have a feminine form and follow the gender of the noun they are modifying. Unlike other adjectives, they can come before or after the noun in the sentence.

Meaning	Sound	Word	Meaning	Sound	Word
1 (f)	khdha	ܚܕܐ	1	kha	ܚܕ
2 (f)	titte	ܬܪܬܝܢ	2	tre	ܬܪܝܢ
3 (f)	tillath	ܬܠܬ	3	tlatha	ܬܠܬܐ
4 (f)	arbe'	ܐܪܒܥ	4	arba	ܐܪܒܥܐ
5 (f)	khammish	ܚܡܫ	5	khamsha	ܚܡܫܐ
6 (f)	ishit	ܫܬ	6	ishta	ܫܬܐ
7 (f)	ishwa'	ܫܒܥ	7	shaw'a	ܫܒܥܐ
8 (f)	tmane	ܬܡܢܐ	8	tmanya	ܬܡܢܝܐ
9 (f)	tisha'	ܬܫܥ	9	tish'a	ܬܫܥܐ
10 (f)	issar	ܥܣܪ	10	isra	ܥܣܪܐ
			11	khadesar	ܚܕܥܣܪ
20	isry	ܥܣܪܝܢ	12	tresar	ܬܪܥܣܪ
30	tlathy	ܬܠܬܝܢ	13	tiltasar	ܬܠܬܥܣܪ
40	arby	ܐܪܒܥܝܢ	14	arbasar	ܐܪܒܥܣܪ
50	khamshy	ܚܡܫܝܢ	15	khamshasar	ܚܡܫܥܣܪ
60	ishty	ܫܬܝܢ	16	ishtasar	ܫܬܥܣܪ
70	shaw'y	ܫܒܥܝܢ	17	ishwashar	ܫܒܥܣܪ
80	tmane	ܬܡܢܝܢ	18	tmanesar	ܬܡܢܥܣܪ
90	tish'y	ܬܫܥܝܢ	19	ichassar	ܬܫܥܣܪ
100	imam	ܡܐܐ	1000	alpa	ܐܠܦܐ

48

Making numbers like 21 is the reverse of the way we do it in English, and is literally "one and twenty:"

ܚܲܕ ܘܐܸܣܪܝܼ

But to say 121, the "hundred" goes first:

ܐܸܡܵܐ ܚܲܕ ܘܐܸܣܪܝܼ

Exercise   ܗܲܪܓܵܐ

---

1. Write the following in English:

2. Write the following in Chaldean:
    A. Your five apples   E. A distant tree
    B. My hungry sister   F. Seventeen pomegranates
    C. Three large apples   G. Her grandson's apricots
    D. Inside the sweet fig   H. A flower from my husband

3. Compose 7 short phrases in Chaldean using the material you've learned so far.

4. Read through the conversation above. Explain the Chaldean words and phrases you understand, and circle the ones you don't understand yet.

Chaldean Culture   ܡܲܪܕܘܼܬܵܐ ܟܲܠܕܵܝܬܵܐ

Figs and dates are two fruits that are considered delicacies to Chaldeans. Eaten fresh, figs can be a refreshing dessert after a large meal. Dried figs are also very common and are sold year round. Dates are also traditionally dried, changing the once yellow fruit to resemble a large raisin. With the pits removed and replaced with walnuts, the dates are now perfect conclusions to any special meal.

Unit 4 Review

1. Write in Chaldean how you would say "Thank you" to the following:

    A. Your brother.
    B. Your sister.
    C. Your parents.

2. Write the following in Chaldean:

A. From your (m) brother	E. Like your (f) nephew
B. His sister	F. Our family
C. Their mother	G. Of her grandfather
D. In my bed	H. And to my paternal uncle

3. Write out all the Possessive Pronouns from memory.

4. Write the following adjectives in their masculine, feminine and plural forms:

ܠ . ܘܟܩܵܕܹܐ   ܐ . ܟܩܘܡܼܐ

ܒ . ܘܕܼܝܩܵܐ   ܒ . ܒܘܼܪܹܟܐ

5. Write out all the masculine numbers from 1-10 from memory.

Story
From the Book of Jonah

Try to figure out as many words as you can in the Chaldean:

And the LORD appointed a great fish to swallow up Jonah; and Jonah was in the belly of the fish three days and three nights. Then Jonah prayed to the LORD his God from the belly of the fish...

ومَدَبّ مُومِبِكَدِّكُ مِنَ بِمِنَ دَنَ
ومِحَتَّلَد لِه هَذَ نَمِنَ، ومِهِومِكَه
نَمِنَ حَدَّهِه دِبِمِنَ هَلَكَ بَمَقَمَ
ومَلَكَ لَبَلَقَهَذَ. ومِم حَدَهِه
دِبِمِنَ مِهِمِلِكِه نَمِنَ نَدِمَ مَدَنَ
دِكُهومِ...

And the LORD spoke to the fish, and it vomited out Jonah upon the dry land.

وقِمِدِكِه مَدَنَ لَبِمِنَ ومِحِمَقِلِد
لِه هَذَ نَمِنَ لَبِتِحَذَ.

Then the word of the LORD came to Jonah the second time, saying, "Arise, go to Nin'eveh, that great city, and proclaim to it the message that I tell you."

وهِومِكَه مَبِنَكَ مَبِمَكَ دِمَدَنَ لَكُهَذَ
دِهِدِهِمِ هَذَ نَمِنَ دِبِمَدَذَ: مومِ
هِد لَبِمِنَذَ مِدِبِمَكَ دَحِكَ ومَحِدِمِ
لِكُه حَدَوومَهَذَ دِبِمَدِقِ كُهِمِقِ.

So Jonah arose and went to Nin'eveh, according to the word of the LORD. Now Nin'eveh was an exceedingly great city, three days' journey in breadth.

وقِمِكِه نَمِنَ ولِكِه لَبِمِنَذَ مِنِ
مَبِنَكَ دِمَدَنَذَ. ومِبِمِنَذَ هِومِومَهَذَ
مِدِبِمَكَ مِبِمَنَذَ دَحِكَ، دَبِمِحَكَ
دِهَلَكَ بَمَقَمَكَ.

Jonah began to go into the city, going a day's journey. And he cried, "Yet forty days, and Nin'eveh shall be overthrown!"

ومِحِمِمَدِبِلِه نَمِنَ لَبِحِدَذَ لَبِمِنَذَ
دَبِمِحَكَ دِبِمَدَ نَمِنَذَ حَمِحَدَهَومِذَ
ومَدِبِمَدَذَ: مِدَهَذَ لَدِدِحِبِ بَمَقَمَكَ
بِمِنَذَ حَمِلَكَذَ.

And the people of Nin'eveh believed God.

وَبِمِنَذَ دِبِمِنَذَ مَهِومِمِهِنَلَكَ دَبِكُهَذَذَ.

Chapter 13
Going to Church;
Personal Pronouns; "to be" Static Present

<table>
<tr><td>**Language**</td><td>لֶشֶّنָא</td></tr>
</table>

Personal Pronouns in English are independent words like "I" and "They." It's the same way in Chaldean, so this chapter is more a matter of memorizing these new words than of understanding a new concept. Here are the "Subjective" (meaning they are the "subject" of the verb) Personal Pronouns:

Meaning	Sound	Pronoun	Meaning	Sound	Pronoun
we	akhny	اֲخְنַن	I	ana	اֲנָא
you (pl)	akhtun	اֲخْתُون	you (m)	ayit	اֲیِت
			you (f)	ayat	اֲیַات
they	any	اֲنِیۇ	he	awu	اֲوُو
			she	ayy	اֲیۡ

If you want to say "I am," it also works just like it does in English – you add a version of the verb "to be." But just like in English, the verb changes depending on the pronoun it's next to – you say "I am," but the verb "am" changes when you say "he is." The same kind of thing happens in Chaldean:

Meaning	Sound	Verb	Meaning	Sound	Verb
we are	y-wukh	اִیۡوُوخ	I am (m)	y-win	اִیۡوִن
			I am (f)	y-wan	اִیۡוַن
you (pl) are	wotun	اִیۡוَאתُون	you (m) are	y-wit	اִیۡוִت
			you (f) are	y-wat	اִیۡوַאت
they are	y-lay	اִیۡלַי	he is	y-lih	اִیۡלִیה
			she is	y-lah	اִیۡלַah

52

You probably noticed that there aren't pronouns on the Chaldean side, only the verb. That's because you don't need them. Just saying *y-lih* means "he is," whether or not you say the pronoun. Of course, it's totally acceptable to say it with the pronoun too:

Meaning	Sound	Phrase	Meaning	Sound	Phrase
we are	*akhny y-wukh*	ܐܲܚܢܲܢ ܐܝܼܘܲܚ	I am (m)	*ana y-win*	ܐܵܢܵܐ ܐܝܼܘܸܢ
			I am (f)	*ana y-wan*	ܐܵܢܵܐ ܐܝܼܘܵܢ
you (pl) are	*akhtun wotun*	ܐܲܚܬܘܼܢ ܐܝܼܘܵܬܘܿܢ	you (m) are	*ayit y-wit*	ܐܲܢ݇ܬ ܐܝܼܘܸܬ
			you (f) are	*ayat y-wat*	ܐܲܢ݇ܬܝ ܐܝܼܘܵܬܝ
they are	*any y-lay*	ܐܵܗܢܝ ܐܝܼܠܹ̈ܝ	he is	*awu y-lih*	ܐܵܗܘ ܐܝܼܠܹܗ
			she is	*ayy y-lah*	ܐܵܗܝ ܐܝܼܠܵܗ̇

Finally, just like in English, this tense of the "to be" verb can be combined with the Infinitive of another verb. For example, the Infinitive of the verb "to walk" is *bi-rkhasha*:

Meaning	Sound	Phrase	Meaning	Sound	Phrase
we are walking	*akhny y-wukh birkhasha*	ܐܝܼܘܲܚ ܒܪ̈ܗܵܛܵܐ	I am (m) walking	*ana y-win birkhasha*	ܐܝܼܘܸܢ ܒܪ̈ܗܵܛܵܐ
			I am (f) walking	*ana y-wan birkhasha*	ܐܝܼܘܵܢ ܒܪ̈ܗܵܛܵܐ
you (pl) are walking	*akhtun wotun birkhasha*	ܐܝܼܘܵܬܘܿܢ ܒܪ̈ܗܵܛܵܐ	you (m) are walking	*ayit y-wit birkhasha*	ܐܝܼܘܸܬ ܒܪ̈ܗܵܛܵܐ
			you (f) are walking	*ayat y-wat birkhasha*	ܐܝܼܘܵܬܝ ܒܪ̈ܗܵܛܵܐ

they are walking	*any y-lay birkhasha*	ܐܝܼܠܹܗ̈ ܒܪܵܚܫܵܐ	he is walking	*awu y-lih birkhasha*	ܐܝܼܠܹܗ ܒܪܵܚܫܵܐ
			she is walking	*ayy y-lah birkhasha*	ܐܝܼܠܵܗ ܒܪܵܚܫܵܐ

Conversation ܡܫܲܥܠܬܵܐ

The Our Father	
Our Father,	ܒܵܒܲܢ ܕܐܝܼܠܹܗ ܒܫܡܲܝܵܐ،
who art in heaven,	ܩܲܕܝܼܫܵܐ ܗܘܵܝܵܐ ܫܡܘܼܟ݂،
hallowed be Thy name.	ܐܵܬܝܵܐ ܡܲܠܟܘܼܬܘܼܟ݂،
Thy kingdom come.	ܗܵܘܹܐ ܨܸܒܝܵܢܘܼܟ݂،
Thy will be done	ܐܲܝܟ ܕܐܝܼܠܹܗ ܒܫܡܲܝܵܐ
on earth as it is in heaven.	ܗܵܕܵܐܝܟ݂ ܗܵܡ ܒܐܲܪܥܵܐ.
Give us this day	ܗܲܒܠܲܢ ܠܲܚܡܵܐ ܕܣܘܿܢܩܵܢܲܢ ܐܵܕܝܘܿܡ.
our daily bread	ܫܒܘܿܩ ܩܵܐܠܲܢ ܚܵܘܒܲܝܢ ܘܚܛܵܗܲܝܢ،
and forgive us our trespasses	ܐܲܝܟ ܕܐܵܦ ܐܲܚܢܲܢ ܫܒܲܩܠܲܢ
as we forgive those	ܠܐ ܐܵܗܵܘ ܕܚܛܹܐܠܗ ܩܵܐܠܲܢ.
who trespass against us.	ܘܠܵܐ ܡܲܥܒܸܪܲܢ ܠܢ ܠܢܸܣܝܘܿܢܵܐ،
And lead us not	ܐܸܠܵܐ ܦܲܨܵܐܠܲܢ ܡܢ ܒܝܼܫܵܐ.
into temptation,	ܡܸܛܠ ܕܝܼܠܘܼܟ݂ ܐܝܼܠܵܗ ܡܲܠܟܘܼܬܵܐ
but deliver us from evil.	ܘܚܲܝܠܵܐ ܘܬܸܫܒܘܿܚܬܵܐ
For thine is the kingdom,	ܠܥܵܠܲܡ ܥܵܠܡܝܼܢ. ܐܵܡܝܼܢ.
the power and the glory,	
Now and forever, amen.	

The Hail Mary

Hail Mary,	ܥܠܰܝܟܝ ܫܠܳܡ ܡܰܪܝܰܡ،
Full of grace,	ܡܰܠܝܰܬ ܛܰܝܒܘܬܐ،
the Lord is with thee.	ܡܳܪܝ ܥܰܡܟܝ،
Blessed art thou	ܡܒܰܪܰܟܬܐ ܐܰܢ̱ܬܝ،
among women,	ܒܢܶܫ̈ܐ،
and blessed is	ܘܰܡܒܰܪܰܟ ܗ̱ܘ
the fruit of thy womb, Jesus.	ܦܺܐܪܐ ܕܟܰܪܣܶܟܝ، ܝܶܫܘܥ.
Holy Mary,	ܩܰܕܺܝܫܰܬ ܡܰܪܝܰܡ،
Mother of God,	ܝܳܠܕܰܬ ܐܰܠܳܗܐ،
pray for us sinners,	ܨܰܠܳܝ ܚܠܳܦܰܝܢ،
now and at the hour	ܚܰܛܳܝ̈ܐ ܗܳܫܐ،
of our death, amen.	ܘܒܫܳܥܬܐ ܕܡܰܘܬܰܢ، ܐܰܡܺܝܢ.

The Glory Be

Glory to the Father,	ܫܘܒܚܐ ܠܐܰܒܐ،
to the Son	ܘܠܰܒܪܐ ܘܰܠܪܘܚܐ ܕܩܘܕܫܐ.
and to the Holy Spirit.	
Forever and ever, amen.	ܡܶܢ ܥܳܠܰܡ ܘܰܥܕܰܡܐ ܠܥܳܠܰܡ ܥܳܠܡܺܝܢ، ܐܰܡܺܝܢ.

Prayer Before Meals

Extend, O Lord our God,	ܦܫܘܛ، ܡܳܪܝܐ ܐܰܠܳܗܰܢ،
the right hand	ܝܰܡܺܝܢܐ ܕܰܡܪܰܚܡܳܢܘܬܟ
of your compassion	
from your holy heaven,	ܡܶܢ ܫܡܰܝܳܐ ܕܩܘܕܫܟ،
and bless this meal	ܘܒܰܪܶܟ ܠܗܳܕܐ ܐܰܟܠܬܐ
of your adorers.	ܕܣܳܓܘܕܰܝܟ ܕܝܠܟ.
Make it abound	ܐܰܣܓܐ ܠܗ̇ ܒܛܳܒ̈ܬܐ ܘܒܘܪ̈ܟܬܐ،
with benefits and blessings	
through the adorable Name	ܒܰܫܡܐ ܣܓܺܝܕܐ
of your glorious Trinity:	ܕܰܬܠܺܝܬܳܝܘܬܟ ܡܫܰܒܰܚܬܐ،
Father, Son	ܐܰܒܐ، ܘܰܒܪܐ،
and Holy Spirit, forever.	ܘܪܘܚܐ ܕܩܘܕܫܐ، ܠܥܳܠܡܺܝܢ.

Vocabulary ܡܝܟ̈ܠܕ

above	forward
ܠܥܝܠ ܡܢ	ܠܩܘܕܡܐ
up	**front**
ܠܥܝܠ	ܩܘܕܡܐ

left		right
ܣܡܠܐ	**Directional Words**	ܝܡܝܢܐ

down	back
ܠܬܚܬ	ܒܣܬܪܐ
under	**backward**
ܬܚܘܬ	ܠܒܣܬܪܐ

Calendar-Related Words

Meaning	Sound	Word
yesterday	*timmal*	ܬܡܠ
today	*idyu*	ܝܘܡܢܐ
tomorrow	*ṣapra*	ܨܦܪܐ
day	*yawma*	ܝܘܡܐ
night	*layli*	ܠܝܠܐ
week	*shabtha*	ܫܒܬܐ
month	*yarkha*	ܝܪܚܐ
season	*shawo'a*	ܫܒܘܥܐ
year	*shata*	ܫܢܬܐ

Days of the Week

Meaning	Sound	Day
Sunday	khoshaba	ܚܕܒܫܒܐ
Monday	turshaba	ܬܪܝܢܒܫܒܐ
Tuesday	thathushaba	ܬܠܬܒܫܒܐ
Wednesday	arbushaba	ܐܪܒܥܒܫܒܐ
Thursday	khamshushaba	ܚܡܫܒܫܒܐ
Friday	'ruta	ܥܪܘܒܬܐ
Saturday	shabtha	ܫܒܬܐ

The Seven Sacraments

Meaning	Sound	Sacrament
Baptism	ma'modytha	ܡܥܡܘܕܝܬܐ
Confirmation	myron	ܡܝܪܘܢ
Confession	mawd'anutha	ܡܘܕܝܢܘܬܐ
Eucharist	qurbana	ܩܘܪܒܢܐ
Marriage	barakhta dzuwagha	ܒܘܪܟܬܐ ܕܙܘܘܓܐ
Ordination	syamydha	ܣܝܡܝܕܐ
Anointing of the Sick	mishha di-kryhi	ܡܫܚܐ ܕܟܪܝܗܐ

Meaning	Sound	Word	Meaning	Sound	Word
altar	madhbha	ܡܕܒܚܐ	bishop	apisqopa	ܐܦܝܣܩܘܦܐ
church	'edta	ܥܕܬܐ	mystery	raza	ܪܐܙܐ
prayer	slotha	ܨܠܘܬܐ	tabernacle	bethid qurbana	ܒܝܬ ܩܘܪܒܢܐ

morning prayer	*sapra*	ܨܦܪܐ	choir	*jwyna*	ܓ̰ܘܝܢܐ
reader	*qaroya*	ܩܪܘܝܐ	rosary	*wardiyya*	ܘܪܕܝܐ
presbyter	*qasha*	ܩܫܐ	much	*kabyra*	ܟܒܝܪܐ
evening prayer	*ramsha*	ܪܡܫܐ	priest	*kahna*	ܟܗܢܐ
deacon	*shamasha*	ܫܡܫܐ	Bible	*kthawa qaddysha*	ܟܬܒܐ ܩܕܝܫܐ

Exercise ܬܡܪܢܐ

1. Write the following in English:

ܐ. ܟܬܒ ܕܫܡܫܢܐ — ܕ. ܨܠܘܬܐ ܩܕܡܝܐ ܡܕܒܚܢܐ

ܒ. ܫܒܥܐ ܡܥܡܘܕܝܬ̈ܐ ܩܕܝܫܬ̈ܐ — ܗ. ܐܢܫܝܢ ܐܝܘܟ ܩܪܘܝܐ

ܓ. ܡܕܒܚܢ̈ܐ ܝܘܡܐ ܕܚܕܒܫܒܐ — ܘ. ܟܗܢܐ ܛܒܐ ܐܝܠܗ

2. Write the following in Chaldean:

A. He is a holy priest
B. Friday is a good day
C. They are walking
D. Tomorrow is Tuesday
E. Six beautiful months
F. You are a great king

3. Compose 7 short phrases in Chaldean using the material you've learned so far.

4. Read through the prayers above. Explain the Chaldean words and phrases you understand, and circle the ones you don't understand yet. Memorize the Our Father.

Chaldean Culture ܟܠܕܝܘܬܐ

Ask a Chaldean what it means to be Chaldean and they will usually say "Catholic." The majority of Chaldeans are Catholic, making it confusing even for them to consider the possibility of non-Catholic Chaldeans. The Chaldean Rite is believed to have been started by St. Thomas the apostle.

Chapter 14
Going Outside;
Demonstratives; Questions; the Imperative

Demonstrative Pronouns are words that refer to things, whether nearby or far away. In English, they are "this" and "these" for nearby things, and "that" and "those" for far away things. It's basically the same in Chaldean, except there are two versions of "that," for masculine and feminine objects (remember that there is no neuter in Chaldean, so nothing can be "it," everything has to be "he" or "she"). The Demonstratives can basically be memorized as vocabulary:

Near	Far	Demonstratives
this ؤَوٖڝ	that (m) ؤَوۨ	Singular
	that (f) ؤَوٝ	
these ؤَوٕڝ	those ؤَوٕڝ	Plural

They are usually used the same way as in English, coming before the noun in the sentence:

ؤَوٕڝ حٮٛڬܬ	ؤَوٝ ܒܚܰܬ̄	ؤَوٖڝ ܓَܒܪܐ
those books	that woman	this man

Question words, or "Interrogative Pronouns," also work just like they do in English, and can be memorized as basic vocabulary:

who	ܡَڝ	where	ܐܝܟَܐ
what	ܡَܘ̈	why	ܐܡ̈ܘ
when	ܐܡَܬ	how	ܕܝ

59

Again, the word order is the same as in English:

ܕܲܝܢ ܐܲܝܟܵܐ؟	ܐܲܝܟܵܐ ܐܝܼܠܲܝ؟	ܡܲܢܘܼ ܐܝܼܠܸܗ؟
how are you?	where are they?	who is he?

The easiest verbal pattern (called a "conjugation") in Chaldean is the Imperative. Imperative verbs are commands. For most verbs, there are only two pieces to the pattern, singular and plural:

do (s)	ܥܒ݂ܘܿܕ
do (pl)	ܥܒ݂ܘܿܕܘ
take (s)	ܫܩܘܿܠ
take (pl)	ܫܩܘܿܠܘ
kill (s)	ܩܛܘܿܠ
kill (pl)	ܩܛܘܿܠܘ

Conversation   ܡܘܼܫܬܲܥܝܼܬ݂ܵܐ

Mariam	During this month of August, the wind is hot.	ܡܲܪܝܲܡ ܒܝܵܪܚܵܐ ܕܐܵܗܵܐ ܕܵܐܒ݂، ܗܵܘܵܐ ܦܵܝܸܫ ܚܲܡܝܼܡܵܐ.
David	Yes, and the trees give many fruits.	ܕܵܘܝܼܕ ܗܹܝ، ܘܐܝܼܠܵܢܹܐ ܝܵܗܒ݂ܝܼ ܦܹܐܪܹܐ ܚܲܒܝܼܪܹܐ.
Mariam	When the clouds come in April, they bring rain with them, and in Summer the earth becomes green and beautiful.	ܡܲܪܝܲܡ ܐܸܡܲܢ ܕܐܵܬ݂ܝܼ ܥܢܵܢܹܐ ܒܢܝܼܣܵܢ، ܡܲܝܬܹܝܢ ܡܸܛܪܵܐ ܥܲܡܲܝܗܝ، ܘܒܩܲܝܛܵܐ ܚܵܦܸܫ ܐܲܪܥܵܐ ܝܘܼܩܢܵܐ ܘܩܘܼܫܒ݂ܬܵܐ.
David	My father says: work the land by day, and sleep at night.	ܕܵܘܝܼܕ ܒܵܒ݂ܝܼ ܐܵܡܸܪ ܐܝܼܬ: ܦܠܘܿܚ ܒܐܲܪܥܵܐ ܒܝܘܿܡܵܐ، ܘܕܡܘܿܟ݂ ܒܠܲܝܠܹܐ.

60

| Mariam | And my mother says to me: study in books, so that you will not see black days. | ܡܿܕܢܼܬ ܘܝܼܡܝ ܚܵܙܡܵܐ ܠܼܝ: ܝܿܩܿܗ ܝܼܚܡܼܬܿ ܗܿܘ ܠܼܐ ܣܿܘܢܹܐ ܢܿܡܵܝܵܐ ܚܿܡܵܐ. |
| David | A white day will come with the snow of winter. | ܘܿܘܹܐ ܚܼܐܹܐ ܢܿܡܵܐ ܣܿܡܵܐ ܠܿܡܹܐ ܗܿܠܼܟܿ ܘܿܗܿܗܵܐ. |

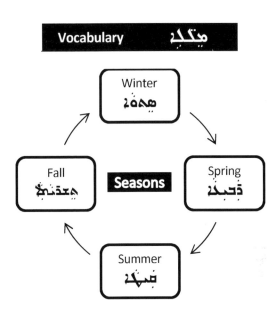

Vocabulary ܡܼܠܼܟ

Winter ܗܿܡܵܐ

Fall ܗܿܥܕܢܿܐ

Seasons

Spring ܕܿܚܼܟܿ

Summer ܩܿܝܼܟܿ

Months of the Year			
Meaning	Month	Meaning	Month
July	ܗܿܡܘܹ	January	ܚܿܢܿ ܬ
August	ܐܿܒ	February	ܝܼܥܬܼܟ
September	ܐܼܠܿܘܠ	March	ܐܿܘܪ
October	ܗܿܥܕܝܼ ܐ	April	ܢܼܣܿܝ
November	ܗܿܥܕܝܼ ܬ	May	ܐܼܝܼܐ
December	ܚܿܢܿ ܐ	June	ܣܿܘܒܿ

61

Weather			
Meaning	**Word**	**Meaning**	**Word**
nice	ܒܣܝܡܐ	rain	ܡܛܪܐ
tepid	ܦܫܘܪܐ	cloud	ܥܢܢܐ
cold	ܩܪܝܪܐ	wind	ܦܘܚܐ
hot	ܚܡܝܡܐ	snow	ܬܠܓܐ

Colors			
Meaning	**Color**	**Meaning**	**Color**
red	ܣܡܘܩܐ	purple	ܐܪܓܝܘܢ
orange	ܦܘܪܬܩܠܢܐ	blue	ܙܪܩܐ
gray	ܩܛܡܢܐ	white	ܚܘܪܐ
yellow	ܫܥܘܬܐ	green	ܝܪܘܩܐ
brown	ܩܘܗܘܝܢܐ	black	ܟܘܡܐ

Imperative Verbs			
Meaning	**Verb**	**Meaning**	**Verb**
do	ܥܒܘܕ، ܥܒܘܕܘܢ	pull	ܓܪܘܫ، ܓܪܘܫܘܢ
run	ܪܗܘܛ، ܪܗܘܛܘܢ	sleep	ܕܡܘܟ، ܕܡܘܟܘܢ
work	ܦܠܘܚ، ܦܠܘܚܘܢ	study	ܕܪܘܫ، ܕܪܘܫܘܢ
listen	ܫܡܘܥ، ܫܡܘܥܘܢ	wear	ܠܒܘܫ، ܠܒܘܫܘܢ
take	ܫܩܘܠ، ܫܩܘܠܘܢ	go down	ܢܚܘܬ، ܢܚܘܬܘܢ

Exercise   ܗܶܢ̈ܐ

1. Write the following in English:

2. Write the following in Chaldean:

A. Red apples in Summer	D. Work the brown earth
B. This is a warm wind	E. Three green trees
C. April is a holy month	F. My father's gray chair

3. Compose 7 short phrases in Chaldean using the material you've learned so far.

4. Read through the conversation above. Explain the Chaldean words and phrases you understand, and circle the ones you don't understand yet.

Chaldean Culture   ܟܠܕܝܘܬܐ

Chaldean time may be comparable to the relaxed standards of South America. Time spent with someone is emphasized more than punctuality, as is characteristic of American culture. Therefore special family gatherings, especially weddings, can typically last long hours into the night.

Chapter 15
Out to Town;
"to have;" "to not have;" "to come"

While many verbs in Chaldean can be complicated to use, some are particularly easy. You already know the "endings" that show possession from Chapter 11. Those same endings are used with the letter *lamadh* and added to verbs to indicate who is doing the action that the verb indicates.

The word *yth* means "there is." If you add this word to a *lamadh* and one of the possessive pronound endings, you create a very common Chaldean idiom: "there is for me," or, in other words, "I have." Here it is piece by piece:

$$ ܐܝܬܠܝ = ܠܝ + ܐܝܬ $$
I have　　*for me*　*there is*

$$ ܐܝܬܠܘܟ = ܠܘܟ + ܐܝܬ $$
you have　　*for you*　*there is*

Notice that the pronunciation silences the *lamadh* and makes the *taw* "hard" rather than "soft." Here's the whole conjugation:

Meaning	Sound	Word
I have	*itt-y*	ܐܝܬܠܝ
you (m, f) have	*itt-ukh, itt-akh*	ܐܝܬܠܘܟ، ܐܝܬܠܟ
he, she has	*itt-ih, itt-ah*	ܐܝܬܠܗ، ܐܝܬܠܗ̇
we have	*itt-an*	ܐܝܬܠܢ
you (pl) have	*itt-okhun*	ܐܝܬܠܘܟ̣ܘܢ
they have	*itt-ay*	ܐܝܬܠܝ

64

To say "I don't have," you add the word *la* to the front, which means "no" or "not." This changes the word in this way:

Meaning	Sound	Word
I don't have	*latt-y*	ܠܸܝܬ݂ܠܝ
you (m, f) don't have	*latt-ukh, latt-akh*	ܠܸܝܬ݂ܠܘܿܟ݂، ܠܸܝܬ݂ܠܵܟ݂
he, she doesn't have	*latt-ih, latt-ah*	ܠܸܝܬ݂ܠܹܗ، ܠܸܝܬ݂ܠܵܗ̇
we don't have	*latt-an*	ܠܸܝܬ݂ܠܲܢ
you (pl) don't have	*latt-okhun*	ܠܸܝܬ݂ܠܵܘܟ݂ܘܿܢ
they don't have	*latt-ay*	ܠܸܝܬ݂ܠܲܝ

So far, this verb (which is "irregular" compared to other verbs, even though it's easy to remember), is in the Present tense. Changing it into other tenses like Past and Future makes things more complicated, and you'll learn that later.

Another verb which is irregular is the verb "to come," but luckily its Past tense is very easy, and very similar to the verb we just learned, so it fits right into this chapter. In this case, the *lamadh* is pronounced:

Meaning	Sound	Word
I came	*the-ly*	ܬܹܐܠܝ
you (m, f) came	*the-lukh, the-lakh*	ܬܹܐܠܘܿܟ݂، ܬܹܐܠܵܟ݂
he, she came	*the-lih, the-lah*	ܬܹܐܠܹܗ، ܬܹܐܠܵܗ̇
we came	*the-lan*	ܬܹܐܠܲܢ
you (pl) came	*the-lokhun*	ܬܹܐܠܵܘܟ݂ܘܿܢ
they came	*the-lay*	ܬܹܐܠܲܝ

Again, don't worry about the other tenses for now.

Conversation ܡܫܥܝܬܐ

Mariam	Welcome, David. This is my cousin George's market.	ܒܫܝܢܐ ܐܬܝܠܘܟ، ܕܘܝܕ. ܐܗܐ ܐܝܠܗ ܫܘܩܐ ܕܒܪܕܕ ܢܫܫܝ، ܓܘܪܓܝܣ.	ܡܪܝܡ
David	How large it is, and full of valuable things!	ܡܐ ܪܒܐ ܐܝܠܗ، ܘܡܠܝܐ ܡܢܕܝܢ̈ܐ ܡܝܩܪܬܐ.	ܕܘܝܕ
Mariam	It has all kinds of clothing, from hats to socks, and from shirts to sandals.	ܐܝܬܠܗ ܓܘܢܢ̈ܐ ܕܟܘܠ ܫܒܠ̈ܐ، ܡܢ ܟܘܦܝ̈ܬܐ ܠܓܪ̈ܒܐ، ܘܡܢ ܫܘܦ̈ܝܬܐ ܠܣܘ̈ܠܐ.	ܡܪܝܡ
David	I don't have a coat. I should buy one now, because they are cheap.	ܐܢܐ ܠܝܬܠܝ ܦܫܘܛ. ܫܘܕ ܙܒܢܢ ܕܗܐ ܚܕܐ، ܡܛܠ ܐܝܠܝ ܐܪܙܘܢ.	ܕܘܝܕ
Mariam	Yes, buy before winter starts and the snow comes down.	ܐܝܢ، ܙܒܘܢ ܩܕܡ ܡܐ ܕܡܫܪܝܐ ܣܬܘܐ ܘܢܚܬ ܬܠܓܐ.	ܡܪܝܡ
David	After we leave, do you want to go to the cinema that is downtown?	ܒܬܪ ܡܐ ܕܦܠܛܘܟ، ܒܥܝܬ ܐܬ ܐܙܠܚ ܠܣܝܢܡܐ ܕܐܝܠܗ ܒܦܠܓܐ ܕܡܕܝܢܬܐ؟	ܕܘܝܕ
Mariam	Yes, I want to, but beforehand I have to fill up my dad's car at the gas station.	ܐܝܢ، ܒܥܝܢ، ܐܠܐ ܩܕܡ ܕܝܢ ܒܡܠܝܢ ܛܢܟܐ ܕܒܒܝ ܒܓܘ ܒܢܙܝܢܟܢܐ.	ܡܪܝܡ
David	If it's expensive, we should go first to the bank.	ܐܢ ܐܝܠܗ ܝܩܪܐ، ܫܘܕ ܐܙܠܚ ܩܕܡܝܐ ܠܒܢܩܐ.	ܕܘܝܕ

Vocabulary ܡܠܹ̈ܐ

Meaning	Word	Meaning	Word
restaurant	ܡܲܛܥܲܡ	expensive	ܝܲܩܘܼܪ
airport	ܡܲܛܵܪ	road	ܐܘܼܪܚܵܐ
cinema	ܣܝܼܢܡܵܐ	cheap	ܙܘܿܠ
car	ܣܲܝܵܪܵܐ	shirt	ܟܘܼܡܘܼ
empty	ܣܦܝܼܩܵܐ	gas station	ܒܢܙܝܼܢܟܵܢܵܐ
pants	ܦܲܛܪܘܿܢ	bank	ܒܲܢܩܵܐ
skirt	ܓܦܢܵܐ	clothes	ܓܘܼܠܹ̈ܐ
simple	ܦܫܝܼܛܵܐ	socks	ܓܘܼܪܒ̈ܐ
house shoes	ܫܘܿܟܹܐ	bridge	ܓܸܫܪܵܐ
robe	ܩܲܒܵܐ	sleepwear	ܕܡܟܬܵܐ
coat	ܩܵܦܘܿܛ	buying	ܙܒܵܢܵܐ
shoe	ܩܘܿܢܕܪܵܐ	belt	ܚܙܵܩܵܐ
market	ܫܘܼܩܵܐ	much	ܟܒܝܼܪܵܐ
dress shirt	ܫܘܿܩܬܵܐ	sandals	ܟܠܟܹ̈ܐ
watch	ܫܵܥܲܬ݂ܵܐ	wallet	ܓܝܼܒܬܵܐ
hat	ܫܲܦܩܵܐ	because	ܡܸܛܠ
dress	ܦܣܛܢܵܐ	city	ܡܕܝܼܢ݇ܬܵܐ

Exercise	ܗܿܢܼ

1. Write the following in English:

ܕ . ܙܒܘܢܝ ܚܘܬܢܐ ܚܠܝܬ݂ܐ ܗܡܙܡܬܐ   ܐ . ܐܸܡܪܟ ܚܙܘܕܫܐ ܕܚܝܟ݂

ܗ . ܥܡܘܟ ܒܟܘܝܟ ܬܿܝܡ ܗܡܘܐ   ܒ . ܙܒܟܘܝ ܗܢܕܐ ܗܡܡܣܡܚ

ܘ . ܡܿܢ ܐܡܐܝܗ ܠܬܝܗ؟   ܓ . ܡܕܝܢܬܿܐ ܐܡܟܬܐ ܬܝܗܕ

2. Write the following in Chaldean:

   A. Three empty cars   D. They don't have apples
   B. The city has one big road E. I came to church today
   C. Who came with you?   F. They have socks and sandals

3. Compose 7 short phrases in Chaldean using the material you've learned so far.

4. Read through the conversation above. Explain the Chaldean words and phrases you understand, and circle the ones you don't understand yet.

Chaldean Culture	ܚܠܕܝܘܬܐ

There are certain spices for cooking, teas, or housing and clothing adornments that are specifically Chaldean and cannot be bought in American superstores. Luckily, in the cities where there are large Chaldean populations there are usually numerous stores that are specifically Middle Eastern. However, nothing beats authenticity, so when Chaldeans travel oversees they usually bring back with them spices or delicacies from the Middle East. It is fun to go into these stores to get a taste of the culture and even practice speaking Chaldean!

Unit 5 Review

1. Write the following in English:

ܐ. ܚܬܝ ܕܝܬܒܢܬ   ܕ. ܦܠܚܗܝ̈ ܬܝܘܡܕ ܚܘܪܢܬ

ܒ. ܣܝܪ̈ܐ ܚܠܡܘܕܝܒܐ ܬܘܝܥܐ   ܗ. ܐܫܢܒ ܙܝܘܘܩ ܚܩܘܝܬ

ܓ. ܣܝܕܬܒܬܐ ܒܗܡܕ ܕܝܕܚܐ   ܘ. ܚܘܢܬ ܗܐܬܐ ܙܒܠܕܗ

2. Write the following in Chaldean:
   - A. Red apples in Summer
   - B. This is a warm wind
   - C. April is a holy month
   - D. Work the brown earth
   - E. Three green trees
   - F. My father's gray chair

3. Recite the Our Father in Chaldean from memory.

4. Write out all the masculine numbers from 1-10 from memory.

5. Write the following in Chaldean from memory:
   - A. I am
   - B. You (m) are
   - C. You (f) are
   - D. He is
   - E. She is
   - F. We are
   - G. You (pl) are
   - H. They are

6. Write the following in Chaldean from memory:
   - A. I have
   - B. You (m) have
   - C. You (f) have
   - D. He has
   - E. She has
   - F. We have
   - G. You (pl) have
   - H. They have

Story

The Policeman and the Thief

Try to figure out as many words as you can in the Chaldean:

A simple man from the villages moved to a new house, and when he was opening one of the closets for clothing, he saw his image in the mirror, and he thought it was a thief. At that moment, he closed the door of the closet, and ran and called a policeman. When they came to the house, they opened the closet, and they both stood in front of the mirror. Then, the policeman said to the man, "Why did you call me, when you [already] have here a policeman who has come to arrest the thief!"

ܚܕ ܓܒܪܐ ܦܫܝܛܐ ܡܢ
ܡܬ̈ܘܬܐ ܡܫܘܢܝܠܗ ܠܒܝܬܐ
ܚܕܬܐ. ܘܟܘܕ ܗܘܐܠܗ
ܒܦܬܚܐ ܚܕ ܡܢ ܕܘܠܒ̈ܐ
ܕܓܘܠܠ̈ܐ ܚܙܐܠܗ ܨܘܪܬܗ
ܒܡܪ̈ܐܝܐ، ܘܚܫܝܒ ܠܗ
ܓܢܒܐ. ܒܝܕܢܗ ܓܠܩܠܗ
ܬܪܥܐ ܕܕܘܠܒܐ، ܘܪܗܛܠܗ
ܩܪܐܠܗ ܚܕ ܫܘܪܛܝ. ܘܟܘܕ
ܐܬܐܠܗ ܠܒܝܬܐ ܦܬܚܠܗ
ܠܕܘܠܒܐ، ܘܩܝܡܠܗ
ܬܪ̈ܘܝܗܘܢ ܩܕܡ ܡܪ̈ܐܝܐ. ܐܗܝ
ܟܗܐ ܐܡܪܠܗ ܫܘܪܛܝ ܠܗ
ܓܒܪܐ: ܐܝܟ ܠܡܢܐ
ܡܩܘܝܬܠܘܟ ܩܠܝ، ܟܘܕ
ܐܝܬܠܘܟ ܐܟܐ ܫܘܪܛܝ ܐܬܝܐ
ܐܗܐ ܠܚܒܝܫܐ ܕܓܢܒܐ!

Poem
Andrew's Song

Try to understand as much as you can, using the Glossary:

Chapter 16
Time for School;
"to go;" "to read;" "to write"

Last chapter you learned the Past tense of the verb "to come." Most Past tense verbs are easy to remember once you have memorized the pattern of "endings" that you saw in that verb. So in this chapter, we'll take what you already know and apply it to the Past tense of three other verbs. The first one is "to go." Just like the verb "to come" that you already learned, "to go" is actually very irregular (and hard to learn) in the Present and Future tenses, but it's very straightforward in the Past tense:

Meaning	Sound	Word
I went	zil-ly	ܙܹܠܠܝ
you (m, f) went	zil-lukh, zil-lakh	ܙܹܠܠܘܟ݂، ܙܹܠܠܵܟ݂
he, she went	zil-lih, zil-lah	ܙܹܠܠܸܗ، ܙܹܠܠܵܗ
we went	zil-lan	ܙܹܠܠܲܢ
you (pl) went	zil-lokhun	ܙܹܠܠܵܘܟ݂ܘܢ
they went	zil-lay	ܙܹܠܠܹܗ

As you see, you use the same endings as you did for "to come" and attach them to the beginning *zil*. For the verb "to read," you do the same with the beginning *qre*:

Meaning	Sound	Word
I read	qre-ly	ܩܪܹܠܝ
you (m, f) read	qre-lukh, qre-lakh	ܩܪܹܠܘܟ݂، ܩܪܹܠܵܟ݂
he, she read	qre-lih, qre-lah	ܩܪܹܠܸܗ، ܩܪܹܠܵܗ

72

we read	*qre-lan*	ܩܪܐ݂ܠܲܢ
you (pl) read	*qre-lokhun*	ܩܪܐ݂ܠܘܟ݂ܘܢ
they read	*qre-lay*	ܩܪܐ݂ܠܗ̈

And the same goes for the verb "to write" (and most other Past tense verbs):

Meaning	Sound	Word
I wrote	*kthu-ly*	ܟܬ݂ܒ݂ܠܝ
you (m, f) wrote	*kthu-lukh, kthu-lakh*	ܟܬ݂ܒ݂ܠܘܟ݂، ܟܬ݂ܒ݂ܠܵܟ݂ܝ
he, she wrote	*kthu-lih, kthu-lah*	ܟܬ݂ܒ݂ܠܹܗ، ܟܬ݂ܒ݂ܠܵܗ̇
we wrote	*kthu-lan*	ܟܬ݂ܒ݂ܠܲܢ
you (pl) wrote	*kthu-lokhun*	ܟܬ݂ܒ݂ܠܘܟ݂ܘܢ
they wrote	*kthu-lay*	ܟܬ݂ܒ݂ܠܗ̈

Conversation ܡܫܲܚܠܦܬܵܐ

Mariam	David, what time is it?	ܕܵܘܝܼܕ، ܟܡܵܐ ܫܵܥܬܼܵܐ ܒܗܵܫܵܐ ܝܼܠܵܗ̇؟	ܡܲܪܝܲܡ
David	It's quarter after 7 in the morning.	ܝܼܠܵܗ̇ ܫܵܥܬܼܵܐ ܕܫܲܒܥܵܐ ܘܪܘܼܒܥܵܐ ܕܨܲܦܪܵܐ.	ܕܵܘܝܼܕ
Mariam	It's time for school	ܥܕܵܢܵܐ ܝܼܠܹܗ ܩܵܐ ܡܲܕܪܲܫܬܵܐ.	ܡܲܪܝܲܡ
David	What time did you go to school yesterday?	ܐܝܼܡܲܢ ܐ݇ܙܸܠܠܵܟ݂ܝ ܠܡܲܕܪܲܫܬܵܐ ܬܡܵܠ؟	ܕܵܘܝܼܕ
Mariam	Yesterday I went at 6:30.	ܬܡܵܠ ܐ݇ܙܸܠܠܝ ܫܵܥܬܼܵܐ ܕܐܸܫܬܵܐ ܘܦܲܠܓܵܐ.	ܡܲܪܝܲܡ

David	Why did you go early yesterday?	ܕܵܘܝܼܕ ܩܵܡܘܿܕܝܼ ܙܲܠܠܲܟ݂ ܩܲܠܘܿܠܵܐ ܬܡܵܠ؟
Mariam	I went early because I read my teacher's book before class.	ܡܲܪܝܲܡ ܙܹܠܠܝܼ ܩܲܠܘܿܠܵܐ ܣܵܒܵܒ ܩܪܹܠܝܼ ܟܬܵܒ݂ܵܐ ܕܡܲܠܦܵܢܝܼ ܩܲܡ ܥܕܵܢܵܐ ܕܝܘܿܠܦܵܢܵܐ .
David	Your teacher wrote a book? How wise he is.	ܕܵܘܝܼܕ ܡܲܠܦܵܢܵܟ݂ ܟܬܝܼܒ݂ܠܹܗ ܟܬܵܒ݂ܵܐ؟ ܟܡܵܐ ܚܲܟܝܼܡܵܐ ܝܼܠܹܗ .
Mariam	He is wise, but he also wants us students to learn well.	ܡܲܪܝܲܡ ܝܼܠܹܗ ܚܲܟܝܼܡܵܐ، ܐܝܼܢܵܐ ܓܲܪܓ ܕܝܼܣܥܝܼ ܐܲܚܢܲܢ ܬܲܠܡܝܼܕܹ̈ܐ ܝܲܠܦܘܿܗ ܨܦܵܝܝܼ .

Vocabulary ܡܹܠܟܹ̈ܐ

Meaning	Word	Meaning	Word
point	ܢܘܿܩܙܵܐ	circle	ܟܸܠܦܵܢܵܐ
line	ܣܸܪܛܵܐ	studying	ܩܪܵܝܬܵܐ
time	ܥܕܵܢܵܐ	paper	ܘܲܪܩܵܐ
page	ܦܵܐܬܵܐ	learning	ܝܘܿܠܦܵܐ
chapter	ܦܵܨܘܿܠܵܐ	school	ܡܲܕܪܲܫܬܵܐ
chalkboard	ܠܘܼܚܵܐ	teacher	ܡܲܠܦܵܢܵܐ
pen	ܩܲܢܝܵܐ	triangle	ܡܬܲܠܬܵܐ
time	ܙܲܒ݂ܢܵܐ	square	ܡܪܲܒܥܵܐ
student	ܬܲܠܡܝܼܕܵܐ	eraser	ܡܲܚܝܵܢܵܐ

Meaning	Word	Meaning	Word
second	ܪܦܦܐ	early	ܩܠܘܠܐ
minute	ܕܩܝܩܐ	late	ܡܥܘܟܒܐ
hour	ܫܥܬܐ	A.M.	ܒܩܘܕܡܬܐ
day	ܝܘܡܐ	P.M.	ܒܬܪ ܦܠܓܝܘܡ

Telling Time			
Masculine #s for Minutes		Feminine #s for Hours	
:01	ܘܚܕ (ܕܩܝܩܐ)	1	ܚܕܐ
:02	ܘܬܪܝܢ (ܕܩܝܩܐ)	2	ܬܪܬܝܢ
:03	ܘܬܠܬܐ ...	3	ܬܠܬ
:04	ܘܐܪܒܥܐ ...	4	ܐܪܒܥ
:05	ܘܚܡܫܐ ...	5	ܚܡܫ
quarter after	ܘܪܘܒܥ	6	ܐܫܬ
:20	ܘܬܠܬ	7	ܐܫܒܥ
half past	ܘܦܠܓܐ	8	ܬܡܢܐ
a third to	ܐܠܐ ܬܠܬ	9	ܬܫܥ
quarter to	ܐܠܐ ܪܘܒܥ	10	ܥܣܪ
:58	ܘܬܡܢܝܐ ܘܚܡܫܝܢ	11	ܚܕܥܣܪ
:59	ܘܬܫܥܐ ܘܚܡܫܝܢ	12	ܬܪܬܥܣܪ

Exercise   ܗܶܢܝܰ

1. Write the following in English:

ܐ. ܘܗܶܡ ܐܶܝܢ   ܒ. ܝܰܬܝܪ ܚܰܡܬܟ ܥܶܦܣܗ؟

ܓ. ܐܘܠܝܗ ܐܬܘܡܝ ܬܡܣܘܥܬܐ   ܗ. ܗܿܡܠܝ ܬܥܝܕܳܢܐ ܕܝܕܝܕ

ܕ. ܚܦܠܝܕܝܣܘܡ ܠܢܬܝ ܐܗܐܠܗ   ܘ. ܬܡܣܘܥܬܐ ܣܕܝܠܒ ܕܝܕܐ

2. Write the following in Chaldean:
     A. 7:20 PM   D. 4:15 PM
     B. This morning at 10:12   E. What time did you read?
     C. I went to school late   F. Your daughter is early

3. Compose 7 short phrases in Chaldean using the material you've learned so far.

4. Read through the conversation above. Explain the Chaldean words and phrases you understand, and circle the ones you don't understand yet.

Chaldean Culture   ܚܠܕܝܣܘܬܐ

The first generation of Chaldean immigrants to America had many highly-educated people, but because of difficulties with transferring degrees that were gained in Iraq, many of them ended up working in stores rather than their original profession. But the value of education never left their hearts, and Chaldean-American children are often encouraged to follow their education as much as possible.

Chapter 17
Food & Kitchen;
"to eat;" "to want"

In this chapter, you'll learn another verb in the Past tense, with the same "endings" as the verbs you've learned already, as well as a new verb with new endings – those that are used in the Present tense (as well as the Future tense, but don't worry about that yet). First, the Past tense of the verb "to eat:"

Meaning	Sound	Word
I ate	khil-ly	ܐܸܟ݂ܠܝܼ
you (m, f) ate	khil-lukh, khil-lakh	ܐܸܟ݂ܠܘܼܟ݂، ܐܸܟ݂ܠܵܟ݂
he, she ate	khil-lih, khil-lah	ܐܸܟ݂ܠܹܗ، ܐܸܟ݂ܠܵܗ
we ate	khil-lan	ܐܸܟ݂ܠܲܢ
you (pl) ate	khil-lokhun	ܐܸܟ݂ܠܵܘܟ݂ܘܿܢ
they ate	khil-lay	ܐܸܟ݂ܠܹܝ

There is a different set of "endings" for the Present tense:

Meaning	Sound	Word
I (m, f) want	kibin, kiban	ܟܹܐܒܼܝܼܢ، ܟܹܐܒܼܵܢ
you (m, f) want	kibit, kibat	ܟܹܐܒܼܝܼܬ، ܟܹܐܒܼܵܬ
he, she wants	kibih, kibah	ܟܹܐܒܼܝܼܗ، ܟܹܐܒܼܵܗ
we want	kibukh	ܟܹܐܒܼܘܼܟ݂
you (pl) want	kibotun	ܟܹܐܒܼܘܿܬܘܿܢ
they want	kibay	ܟܹܐܒܼܝܼ

While the verb "to want" isn't totally regular, the endings of the Present tense are basically what you'd expect with other verbs. For now, memorize the pattern for this verb, since it's pretty commonly used.

Conversation ܡܿܣܒܚܝܬ݂ܐ

Mariam	What do you want to eat, David? Are you hungry?	ܡܸܪܝܲܡ ܡܸܐ ܒܲܥܝܸܬ݂ ܗ̇ܿܝ ܒܝܼܟ݂ܲܠܵܐ، ܕܵܘܝܼܕ؟ ܒܝܼܘܸܗ ܟܦܝܼܢܵܐ؟
David	Yes. I want dolma. Do you have any?	ܕܵܘܝܼܕ ܗܹܢ. ܐܵܢܵܐ ܒܲܥܝܸܢ ܕܘܼܠܡܹܐ. ܐܝܼܬ݂ܠܵܘܟ݂ܘܼܢ؟
Mariam	No. We have rice and *maraqa*.	ܡܸܪܝܲܡ ܠܵܐ. ܐܝܼܬ݂ܠܲܢ ܪܸ݂ܙܵܐ ܘܡܲܪܲܩܵܐ.
David	Rice and *maraqa* are also tasty.	ܕܵܘܝܼܕ ܗܹܡ ܪܸ݂ܙܵܐ ܘܡܲܪܲܩܵܐ ܒܝܼܠܹܐ ܛܲܥܝܼܡܹܐ.
Mariam	After eating, do you want to drink tea?	ܡܸܪܝܲܡ ܒܵܬ݂ܲܪ ܒܝܼܟ݂ܲܠܵܐ، ܒܲܥܝܸܬ݂ ܕܬܲܥܡܸܗ ܟ݂ܵܝ؟
David	Yes, I do.	ܕܵܘܝܼܕ ܗܹܢ، ܒܲܥܝܸܢ.
Mariam	Do you want sugar with your tea?	ܡܸܪܝܲܡ ܟܸܡܝܵܕ ܟ݂ܵܝ ܒܲܥܝܸܬ݂ ܥܲܢܵܐ؟
David	No, honey is more tasty with tea.	ܕܵܘܝܼܕ ܠܵܐ. ܕܸܒ݂ܫܵܐ ܒܸܫ ܛܲܥܝܼܡܵܐ ܒܝܼܠܹܗ ܟܸܡܝܵܕ ܟ݂ܵܝ.
Mariam	Anything you like!	ܡܸܪܝܲܡ ܟܲܠ ܕܹܒ݂ ܘܒܝܼܣ.

Vocabulary ܡܸܠܹ̈ܐ

Meaning	Word	Meaning	Word
spoon	ܡܲܓܪܲܦܬܵܐ	teacup	ܦܝܼܢܓܵܢ
water	ܡܝܵܐ	egg	ܒܹܥܬܵܐ
sink	ܡܲܓܗܲܠܬܵܐ	biryani	ܒܸܪܝܵܢܝ
salt	ܡܸܠܚܵܐ	cheese	ܓܘܼܒܬܵܐ
pan	ܡܲܣܠܬܵܐ	bulgar wheat	ܓܘܼܪܓܘܼܪ
stew	ܡܲܪܲܩܵܐ	rolling pin	ܓܪܘܼܡܵܐ
knife	ܣܲܟܝܼܢܵܐ	honey	ܕܸܒܫܵܐ
meat	ܒܸܣܪܵܐ	dolma	ܕܘܼܠܡܵܐ
barley	ܦܣܘܬܐ	pot	ܕܝܼܣܬܵܐ
stove	ܓܪܝ	yogurt	ܚܲܠܒܵܐ
plate	ܦܝܼܢܟܵܐ	milk	ܚܠܝܵܐ
platter	ܦܝܼܢܓܵܢ	wine	ܚܲܡܪܵܐ
teapot	ܩܘܼܪܝܼ	cup	ܟܵܣܵܐ
rice	ܪܘܼܙܵܐ	tea	ܟܵܝ
sugar	ܫܲܟܲܪ	serving spoon	ܟܲܡܟܵܐ
cheese pie	ܒܘܼܪܹܟܬܵܐ	fork	ܟܲܢܓܲܠ
refrigerator	ܬܠܓܐ	bread	ܠܲܚܡܵܐ

Exercise ܡܘܼܪܵܢܵܐ

1. Write the following in English:

ܐ. ܐܝܼܬ ܒܹܥܬܵܐ ܚܲܡܪܵܐ

ܒ. ܐܲܟܠܘܼܟ ܪܘܼܙܵܐ ܡܢ ܬܠܓܐ

ܓ. ܐܲܟܠܘܼܢ ܚܲܠܒܵܐ ܘܕܸܒܫܵܐ

ܕ. ܠܲܚܡܵܐ ܘܓܘܼܒܬܵܐ ܘܟܵܝ

ܗ. ܡܵܐ ܐܲܟܠܠܗ ܐܲܣܝܘܼܪܝ؟

ܘ. ܐܝܼܬ ܡܲܪܲܩܵܐ ܓܵܘ ܕܝܼܣܬܵܐ

2. Write the following in Chaldean:
   A. They ate the bread   D. Do you want a large spoon?
   B. I want sugar with my tea   E. How much did she eat?
   C. He ate with a fork   F. Bread, cheese and watermelon

3. Compose 7 short phrases in Chaldean using the material you've learned so far.

4. Read through the conversation above. Explain the Chaldean words and phrases you understand, and circle the ones you don't understand yet.

Chaldean Culture   ܟ݁ܠܕ݂ܝܡܘܬ݂ܐ

Chaldean cuisine is representative of a Middle Eastern diet. *Maraqa*, a vegetable-based stew with meat is standard for an everyday dinner meal, served with rice. *Gurgur* (barley), rice, and pita are grains used in many of the meals. *Hummus, tabbulah* (parsley salad), and *turshy* (spicy pickled vegetables) are usually served alongside *dolma* (stuffed grape leaves), *biryani* (seasoned rice and lamb with rice and vegetables) or *patcha* (stuffed lamb instestine) for a more formal meal.

Chapter 18
Animals & Feelings;
"to do"

You may have noticed in the last chapter that the Present tense of the verb "to want" begins with a *kap*. This letter is at the beginning of all Present tense verbs, and it's the tell-tale sign that you're looking at the Present tense. Letters like this (or combinations of letters) are called "tense indicators." So you shouldn't be surprised to see a *kap* at the beginning of the Present tense of the verb "to do:"

Meaning	Sound	Word
I (m, f) do	kawdhin, kawdhan	ܟܵܘܕܸܢܿ، ܟܵܘܕܸܢ
you (m, f) do	kawdhit, kawdhat	ܟܵܘܕܸܬܿ، ܟܵܘܕܸܬ
he, she does	kawidh, kawdha	ܟܵܘܕܸ، ܟܵܘܕܵܐ
we do	kawdhukh	ܟܵܘܕܘܿܟ݂
you (pl) do	kawdhutun	ܟܵܘܕܘܿܬܘܿܢ
they do	kawdhy	ܟܵܘܕܝ

This verb, "to do," happens to be fairly "regular," which means the pattern that it exhibits applies to most verbs. So you should spend some time memorizing the endings that you see in the chart above, since they are found in a lot of places in the Chaldean language, especially in verbs.

In addition to the *kap* being the Present tense indicator, it's worthwhile to learn, as this book comes to a close and you get ready to study the Grammar in the next book, the Future tense indicator, which is the particle *bid*. This sound goes at the beginning of the word, with the same endings as the Present tense, and you get the Future tense:

Meaning	Sound	Word
I (m, f) will do	bidawdhin, bidawdhan	ܒܸܕܲܘܕܹܢ، ܒܸܕܲܘܕܵܢ
you (m, f) will do	bidawdhit, bidawdhat	ܒܸܕܲܘܕܹܬ، ܒܸܕܲܘܕܵܬ
he, she will do	bidawidh, bidawdha	ܒܸܕܲܘܸܕ، ܒܸܕܲܘܕܵܐ
we will do	bidawdhukh	ܒܸܕܲܘܕܘܼܟ݂
you (pl) will do	bidawdhutun	ܒܸܕܲܘܕܘܼܬܘܿܢ
they will do	bidawdhy	ܒܸܕܲܘܕܝܼ

Just like the *kap* indicating the Present tense, *bid* applies to all kinds of verbs, so it's something worth remembering.

You already have a good idea of how to make a Past tense verb, but here's the Past tense of "to do" just so you have a complete picture of how regular verbs work:

Meaning	Sound	Word
I did	'widh-ly	ܘܼܕܹܠܝܼ
you (m, f) did	'widh-lukh, 'widh-lakh	ܘܼܕܹܠܘܿܟ݂، ܘܼܕܹܠܵܟ݂
he, she did	'widh-lih, 'widh-lah	ܘܼܕܹܠܹܗ، ܘܼܕܹܠܵܗ
we did	'widh-lan	ܘܼܕܹܠܲܢ
you (pl) did	'widh-lokhun	ܘܼܕܹܠܵܘܟ݂ܘܿܢ
they did	'widh-lay	ܘܼܕܹܠܲܝ

Conversation ܡܲܡܠܠܐ

Mariam	What does a bear do with a fish?	ܡܸܪܝܲܡ ܡܐ ܟܹܐ ܥܵܒܹܕ ܕܸܒܵܐ ܥܲܡ ܢܘܼܢܵܐ؟
David	The bear eats the fish.	ܕܵܘܝܼܕ ܗܵܐ ܕܸܒܵܐ ܟܹܐ ܐܵܟܹܠ ܠܹܗ ܠ ܢܘܼܢܵܐ.
Mariam	And what did the tiger do to the tired lion?	ܡܸܪܝܲܡ ܘܡܐ ܡܘܼܕܹܐ ܠܹܗ ܒܲܒܪܵܐ ܗܵܐ ܐܲܪܝܵܐ ܡܲܟ݂ܝܵܢܵܐ؟
David	The tiger killed the tired lion.	ܕܵܘܝܼܕ ܒܲܒܪܵܐ ܩܛܝܼܠܹܗ ܗܵܐ ܐܲܪܝܵܐ ܡܲܟ݂ܝܵܢܵܐ.
Mariam	And what happened to the hen when the elephant stepped on her?	ܡܸܪܝܲܡ ܘܡܐ ܗܘܹܐ ܠܹܗ ܗܲܡܙܘܼܡܹܐ ܟܲܕ ܕܝܼܫܠܹܗ ܥܠܹܗ ܦܝܼܠܵܐ؟
David	The hen died and the rooster cried for her.	ܕܵܘܝܼܕ ܩܲܡܝܵܢ ܡܝܼܬܠܵܗ، ܘܒܸܟ݂ܝܵܐ ܬܸܪܢܓ݂ܠܵܐ ܥܠܵܗ.
Mariam	What will the dog do if he sees a happy cat?	ܡܸܪܝܲܡ ܡܐ ܒܸܕ ܥܵܒܹܕ ܟܲܠܒܵܐ ܐܸܢ ܚܵܙܹܐ ܠܹܗ ܗܵܐ ܩܵܛܘܼ ܒܲܣܝܼܡܬܵܐ؟
David	The dog will become angry and will run after her.	ܕܵܘܝܼܕ ܟܲܠܒܵܐ ܒܸܕ ܦܵܝܹܫ ܣܸܡܚܵܢܵܐ ܘܒܸܪܚܵܛܵܐ ܒܵܬܪܵܗ.
Mariam	If a monkey laughed at a dragon, what happened to him?	ܡܸܪܝܲܡ ܐܸܢ ܡܸܩܪܵܐ ܓ݂ܵܚܸܟ݂ܠܹܗ ܥܲܠ ܗܲܒܝܼܢܵܐ، ܡܐ ܗܘܹܐ ܠܹܗ ܐܸܠܹܗ؟
David	100% he burned in fire and laughs no more.	ܕܵܘܝܼܕ ܐܸܡܵܐ ܒܐܸܡܵܐ ܝܩܝܼܕܠܹܗ ܒܢܘܼܪܵܐ ܘܠܵܐ ܩܲܬ ܓ݂ܵܚܸܟ݂.

Vocabulary ܡ̈ܠܐ

Feelings			
Meaning	**Word**	**Meaning**	**Word**
hurt	ܡܪܝܥܐ	surprised	ܬܡܝܗܬܐ
embarrassed	ܢܟܝܦܐ	tired	ܓܘܢܐ
upset	ܟܡܝܪܐ	dizzy	ܓܝܓܐ
happy	ܦܨܝܚܐ	angry	ܚܡܝܡܢܐ
sad	ܡܥܝܩܐ	suffering	ܚܫܝܫܐ
feverish	ܫܚܝܢܐ	sick	ܟܪܝܗܐ

Animals			
Meaning	**Word**	**Meaning**	**Word**
fish	ܢܘܢܬܐ	lion	ܐܪܝܐ
tiger	ܢܡܪܐ	duck	ܒܛܐ
eagle	ܢܫܪܐ	flea	ܒܩܐ
rat	ܥܘܩܒܪܐ	wolf	ܕܐܒܐ
rabbit	ܐܪܢܒܐ	bear	ܕܒܐ
elephant	ܦܝܠܐ	bee	ܕܒܫܐ
frog	ܦܩܐ	fly	ܕܝܕܘܐ
cat	ܩܛܘܬܐ	rooster	ܕܝܟܐ
turtle	ܩܪܓܠܐ	blackbird	ܦܘܢܕܐ
monkey	ܩܪܕܐ	donkey	ܚܡܪܐ
bull	ܬܘܪܐ	dove	ܝܘܢܐ
cow	ܬܘܪܬܐ	dog	ܟܠܒܐ
dragon	ܬܢܝܢܐ	hen	ܟܬܝܬܐ

Exercise	ܗܿܦܟܼܐ

1. Write the following in English:

ܒ . ܗܸܘܵܕܵܐ ܡܝܼܠܸܗ ܡܸܕܘܼܪܵܐ   ܐ . ܙܵܩܢܵܐ ܟܼܒܼܫܵܐ ܡܸܢ ܬܸܩܢܵܐ

ܗ . ܗܿܘܹܐ ܒܥܹܕܵܐ ܡܕܒܼܟܼܵܐ   ܬ . ܝܼܗܘܵܐ ܟܼܒܼܝܼ ܥܲܠܡܵܐ

ܘ . ܒܸܪܵܐ ܐܹܟܼܠܸܗ ܟܡܝܼܫܹܐ   ܟ . ܒܸܬ ܗܿܡܸܣܥܸܒ ܒܼܬܼܢܵܐ

2. Write the following in Chaldean:
   A. Four embarrassed hens   D. A sick lion and a happy cow
   B. The rooster did good   E. Why did the eagle come?
   C. The bear will eat the fish   F. Dragons eat hens

3. Compose 7 short phrases in Chaldean using the material you've learned so far.

4. Read through the conversation above. Explain the Chaldean words and phrases you understand, and circle the ones you don't understand yet.

Chaldean Culture	ܟܠܕܵܝܘܼܬܵܐ

Moving from Iraq to the United States is not easy, but moving to areas where there are already many Chaldeans makes the transition easier. Detroit and San Diego are two cities where there are large populations of Chaldeans, but many Chaldeans also live in Arizona, Las Vegas, Chicago, Texas and Northern California.

Unit 6 Review

1. Write the following in English:

ܕ. ܡܒܥ ܚܘܝܠܟ ܥܡܣܗ؟   ܘ. ܙܥܡ ܘܗܠܗ

ܗ. ܙܘܠܠܗ ܠܥܘܡܢ ܬܥܣܘܥܬܐ   ܘ. ܗܡܠ ܚܥܕܢܓ ܕܙܕܬ

ܠ. ܚܦܠܝܕܝܘܡ ܠܢܬܢ ܙܗܙܠܗ   ܘ. ܬܥܣܘܥܬܐ ܡܕܙܠܒ ܕܒܕܙ

2. Write the following in Chaldean:
   - A. They ate the bread
   - B. I want sugar with my tea
   - C. He ate with a fork
   - D. Do you want a large spoon?
   - E. How much did she eat?
   - F. Bread, cheese and watermelon

3. Recite the Hail Mary in Chaldean from memory.

4. Write out all the feminine numbers from 1-10 from memory.

5. Write the following in Chaldean from memory:
   - A. I ate
   - B. You (m) ate
   - C. You (f) ate
   - D. He ate
   - E. She ate
   - F. We ate
   - G. You (pl) ate
   - H. They ate

6. Write the following in Chaldean from memory:
   - A. I will do
   - B. You (m) will do
   - C. You (f) will do
   - D. He will do
   - E. She will do
   - F. We will do
   - G. You (pl) will do
   - H. They will do

Story
The Donkey, Head Builder

Try to figure out as many words as you can in the Chaldean:

A herd of many animals wanted to move from its place to another place more filled with grass and greenery. While they were walking, they reached a river, and the animals voted to build a bridge over it. They chose the donkey to be the head builder. Then the donkey gathered the whole herd together, and opened the meeting and said: Thank you for your faith in me. But before we begin building, I must know: how would you like the bridge to cross the river, horizontally or vertically?

سِיֹּدَ֞ حۅܡܕܵ؟ ܕۡحۡحۡܒܕ؟ ܣܬܢܿهܒ
حۡܒܬܟܵ؟ هֹܘ؟ ܕۡܡܥܡܢܵ؟ هֹܘ؟؟
ܡܢ ܕۅ؟ܚۡهֹܗ ܠܣۡܒܕَهۡ؟ ܕۅܚܕ܊
ܬܕ ܗֻܕۡهַ ܠܟܠ ܡۡܒܿܡۡۅهַهَ؟.
ۅحۅܡ ܠֹهֹܒ ܒۡܕܣۡܙֹܬ ܗܩܒܝ؟ܟ
ܡֻܕܡۡܓ ܣܢܿܝ ܕَهֹܕ؟،، ۅܣۡܡֻܬܢ
ܕܦ؟ܟܕ ܕَܢ܊ܒ ܗۡܕ ܬ̈ܒܡ ܠ̈ܥܕَ؟
ܒ̈ܠܿهַ. ۅܡܩܝܡۅܬ؟ܟܕ ܣܡֻܕَ؟
ܗۡܕ هَܘ؟ ܕَܥَܕ ܕَܬܢܿܝܬ. هַܡܠَهَ؟
ܣܡֻܕَ؟ ܠ̈ܣܝܠܠ̈ܝ ܚۅܟ̇ה
حۅ؟ܡܕَ؟، ۅܩֻ؟ܣۡܠ̈ܝ ܒۡ̈ܒܚ̈ܬܓ
ۅ؟ܗܕَܟ̇ܝ: ܠܢܬ̇ۅۡܗۅ܊
ܬܣܝܡܡ̈ܝ ܠ̈ܟ هַ؟ܡֻܢۡܡۅ܊ۅۡهۅ܊
ܬܠ̈ܝܡ܊. ܬ̇ܢ ܣֻ؟ܡܡֻܕَ؟
ܕَܡܥَܬ؟ۅۡ؟ ܒ̈ܬܢ̈ܝ؟ ܗܠ̈ۅ؟ܡܕَ؟
ܕَܢֻ܊ܝܟ: ܕَ؟ܒܝ ܚ̈ܒܬܠ̈ܗۅۡهۅ܊
ܠֹܗ ܠ̈ܥܕَ؟: ܬܩۡ̈ܝܡۅۡ̈ܘۡ̈ܝ ܕَ؟ܕَهֹܕَ؟
ܢֻ܊ ܒ̈ܒܕَۅ̈ܣۅۡهۅ܊؟!

Poem
Hymns of Exaltation

Try to understand as much as you can, using the Glossary:

89

91

RTL

93

ܘܗܕܐܝܟ ܡܢ ܙܒܢܐ ܕܫܩܠܗܝ ܡܠܟܐ، ܗܕܝܟ ܠܫܢܐ ܗܘܝܢ ܗܘܐ ܡܫܘܦܠܝܐ ܒܒܝܬ ܢܗܪܝܢ: ܐܟܕܝܐ ܐܦ ܫܘܡܪܝܐ ܘܦܘܡܪܝܐ ܡܠܟܝܐ، ܘܐܬܘܪܝܐ ܐܦ ܡܫܝܚܝܬܐ ܘܬܘܟܠܬܐ ܘܫܩܠܬܐ ܘܡܕܝܢܬܐ.

ܟܠܕܝܐ، ܕܗܘܝ ܗܘܐ ܚܕ ܫܒܛܐ ܐܪܡܝܐ، ܟܕ ܡܠܝܟܠܗ ܥܠ ܒܒܠ، ܠܫܢܐ ܐܪܡܝܐ ܒܪ ܦܝܫܠܗ ܘܒܣܡܠܗ ܥܠ ܕܦܝܫܠܗ ܠܫܢܐ ܐܪܡܝܐ ܕܒܝܬ ܢܗܪܝܢ ܘܕܫܘܪܝܐ ܘܦܠܫܛܝܢ ܘܠܫܢܐ ܕܬܘܟܠܬܐ ܘܫܩܠܬܐ ܕܬܫܡܫܬܐ ܒܝܬ ܡܠܟܘܬܐ ܕܗܘܠܗ ܡܕܝܢܬܐ ܡܝܬܢܐ. ܘܗܕܐܝܟ ܕܫܠܛܠܗ ܥܠ ܫܢܬܐ ܕ331 ܩ.ܡ. ܟܕ ܐܠܟܣܢܕܪ ܡܩܕܘܢܝܐ ܟܒܫܠܗ ܠܒܒܠ ܘܡܢ ܗܘ ܙܒܢܐ ܗܘ ܝܘܢܝܐ ܦܝܫܠܗ ܡܢ ܠܫܢܐ ܕܬܫܡܫܬܐ ܒܝܬ ܡܠܟܘܬܐ ܕܡܕܝܢܬܐ، ܟܕ ܐܪܡܝܐ ܦܝܫܠܗ ܕܘܟܬܗ ܡܢ ܠܫܢܐ ܥܡܡܝܐ ܕܥܡܐ.

ܒܫܢܬܐ ܩܠܘܡܐ ܕܝܫܘܥ، ܕܠܫܢܐ ܐܪܡܝܐ ܐܝܬܘܗܘܐܝܗ ܠܫܢܐ ܡܫܘܚܠܦܐ. ܚܕ ܗܘܐܗܘܐ ܠܫܢܐ ܕܒܒܠ، ܐܚܪܢܐ ܗܘܐܗܘܐ ܠܫܢܐ ܕܐܘܪܗܝ، ܘܐܚܪܢܐ ܕܗܘܕܝܐ ܢܐ ܕܦܠܫܛܝܢ. ܒܝܬܐ ܕܡܕܝܢܐ ܘܡܕܝܢܬܐ ܡܫܘܚܠܦܬܐ ܒܐܬܪܘܬܐ ܘܕܘܟܝܬܐ ܕܝܠܗ ܠܫܢܐ ܕܐܘܪܗܝ، ܕܦܝܫܠܗ ܝܕܝܥܐ ܣܘܪܝܝܐ، ܟܕ ܠܫܢܐ ܐܪܡܝܐ ܕܥܡܐ، ܦܝܫܠܗ ܗܘ ܡܫܝܚܝܐ ܘܡܫܘܚܠܦܐ ܥܠ ܗܕܝܘܬ ܗܘܐ ܦܪܫܝܢܝܐ ܗܘܝܢܐ ܒܐܪܡܝܐ.

ܩܝܨܐ ܕܚܠܝܢܐ ܢܝܨܝܢܐ
ܕܡܩܪܠܝܗ ܠܙܗܕܝܨܐ

ܥܠܡܐ ܕ 1905، ܪܕܒ ܢܝܠܗܐ، ܪܒܬܝܕ ܒܥܢܐܢܐ ܣܘܪܠܝܗ
ܬܥܝܠܪܢܝܢܐ ܕܗܗܪܕܝܢ ܢܗܐܠܝܢܝܢ ܩܡܝܕܝܒܠܐ ܕܝܢܠܕ ܣܝܪܝ
ܚܡܝܬܐ، ܕܝܝܨܩܪܗܗ ܠܐܢ ܬܠܗܘܕ ܡܝܠܠܝܗ ܢܠ ܡܥܕܝܒܐ ܗܪ
ܬܪܢܗ ܥܠܡܐ، ܣܥܒܪܐ ܪܢܐܗ ܚܡܝܬܐ: ܗܝܪܝܨܝ. ܩܝ ܗܝܪܝܢܝܢ
ܠܥܢܠܕ ܚܡܝܬܝ ܪܪܝܝܢ ܪܝܢܝ ܪܝܢܝ ܢܥܪ ܚܠܝܢܐ ܗܝܡܝܠܢܐ ܢܠ ܣܝܪܩܝܗ
ܬܠܠܥܪ ܪܝܢܝ ܥܠܡܐ ܕ 1668 ܗ 1680.

ܗܪ ܠܝܪܥܪ ܠܝܪܝܠܝܗ ܡܢܠܝܬܠܐ ܗܪ ܢܐ ܗܗ ܪܚܢܪܝܕ
ܨܥܪܒܢܐ ܕܬܬܢܡܝ، ܕܩܡܝܢܠܕ ܠܝܢܝܕܝܗܢܝ ܩܝܒ ܗܗܝܬܝܗ
ܗܠܢܩ. ܠܝܨܝܪ ܢܐܗܝܪܒ ܗܪ ܚܣܘܗܥ ܠܝܗ ܩܝܢܝܒ ܪܪܬ ܪܝܢܝ ܠܝܪܪܝ
ܩܝܡ ܠܥܢܐ ܪܝܠܝ ܗܩܝܪ ܢܗܪܝ ܢܗܢܝ ܗܝܪܝܣܢܐ ܗܗܪܠܝܪܗܗ ܪܩܡܝܪ
ܠܙܗܕܝܒܐ ܩܝܡ ܥܢܐ ܕ 1670. ܥܒܥܪ ܪܗܪ ܚܠܝܢܐ ܪܝܠܝܗ: ܢܥܪ
ܪܠܢܗ ܗܝܡܝܠܢܐ.

ܢܥܪ ܢܠ ܚܗܪܒ ܪܠܢܗ، ܠܝܪܪܐ ܗܪܐ ܠܝܥܪ ܗܗܥܪ ܣܗܬܐ ܗܪ
ܣܝܪܝܨ، ܥܥܣܢܠܝܗ ܝܠܝܪܪ ܥܠܡܐ ܕ 1668 ܗܥܝܢܐ ܠܥܨܝܠܠܝܗ ܗܪ
ܪܗܪܢܥܠܝܕ. ܗܝܥܐܪܥܪ ܪܗܪܪܢܠܝܗ ܢܥܬܪܗ ܪܝܥܪܪܝ ܪܗܠܠܝܗ ܠܝܢܠܕ
ܗܥܝܢܐ ܠܐܠܠܝܨܥܝܪܪܥܢܝܢܝ. ܗܩܝܡ ܢܗܝܥܝܪܪܥܢܝܢܐ ܗܗܡܗܝܨܪܠܝܗ ܪܪܗܗܪܢܐ
ܪܢܥܪ ܠܠܝܝܝܝܗܢܐ، ܗܥܝܢܐ ܡܚܗܡܝܠܠܝܗ ܗܢܠ ܠܪܪܝܥܪ ܗܪܝܗܥܢܐ.
ܚܗܪ ܚܗܪܒ ܪܠܢܗ ܥܠܝܢܠܝܗ ܠܪܝܗܥܢܐ، ܗܪ ܢܗܪܪ ܢܝܥܪ ܪܥܗܪܥܗܪ
ܝܠܗܢܐ ܬܥܥܥܗܗܥܪܪ ܠܝܥܥܢܐ ܪܝܠܠܥܪ ܢܝܪܥܪ: ܢܪܗܕܝܒܐ.

97

99

Chaldean – English Glossary

ܐ

August ܐܒ

father ܐܒܐ

abbot ܐܒܐ، ܐܒܒܐ

destruction ܐܒܕܢܐ

avocado ܐܒܘܟܕܐ

priest, "father" ܐܒܘܢܐ

silk ܐܒܪܝܫܡ

hired servant ܐܓܝܪܐ

fee ܐܓܪܐ

roof, terrace ܐܓܪܐ

expensive ܐܓܪܝ

epistle ܐܓܪܬܐ

post office ܐܓܪܬܐ

today ܐܕܝܘܡ، ܗܕܝܘܡ

March ܐܕܪ

this ܐܗܕܐ، ܐܗܕܝ

that (m) ܐܗܘ، ܐܗܘ

he, she ܐܗܘ، ܐܗܝ

that (f) ܐܗܝ، ܐܗܝ

these ܐܗܠ، ܐܗܢܝ

they ܐܗܢܝ

those ܐܗܢܝ

dining room ܐܘܕܐ ܕܐܟܠܐ

family room ܐܘܕܐ ܕܐܝܡܬܐ

bedroom ܐܘܕܐ ܕܕܡܟܐ

alas ܐܘܝ

lamentation, elegy ܐܘܠܝܬܐ

affliction ܐܘܠܨܢܐ

nation ܐܘܡܬܐ

manager ܐܘܡܢܐ، ܐܘܡܢܐ

male ܐܘܪܙܐ

road, way ܐܘܪܚܐ

bus route ܐܘܪܚܐ ܕܒܣ

crosswalk ܐܘܪܚܐ ܕܪܚܫܐ

highway ܐܘܪܚܐ ܦܫܝܛܬܐ

traveler ܐܘܪܚܢܐ

Old Testament ܐܘܪܝܬܐ

stole ܐܘܪܪܐ

flat iron ܐܘܬܝ

go ܐܙܠ، ܐܝܙܠ

goer ܐܙܠܐ

brother ܐܚܐ، ܐܚܘܢܐ

siblings ܐܚܘܢܘܬܐ

brotherhood ܐܚܘܬܐ

we ܐܚܢܢ

last, hindmost ܐܚܪܝܐ

English	Chaldean	English	Chaldean
other, another, again	ܐܚܪܸܢܵܐ	but, yet	ܐܸܠܵܐ
hand	ܐܝܼܕܵܐ	God	ܐܲܠܵܗܵܐ
sitting room	ܐܲܝܘܵܢ	Divinity	ܐܲܠܵܗܘܼܬ݂ܵܐ
ambassador, messenger	ܐܝܼܙܓܲܕܵܐ	divine	ܐܲܠܵܗܵܝܵܐ
about, nearly	ܐܲܝܟ݂	street	ܐܘܼܠܵܨܵܐ
like, according, as, where	ܐܲܝܟ݂ܵܐ	narrow	ܐܲܠܝܼܨܵܐ
location	ܐܲܝܟܵܘܼܬ݂ܵܐ	thousand	ܐܵܠܸܦ
food	ܐܝܼܟܼܠܵܐ	thousandth	ܐܲܠܦܵܝܵܐ
responsibility	ܐܝܼܟܼܠܵܐ ܕܝܼܠܹܗ	hundred	ܐܸܡܵܐ
September	ܐܝܼܠܘܼܠ	amen	ܐܵܡܹܝܢ
tree	ܐܝܼܠܵܢܵܐ	perpetually	ܐܲܡܝܼܢܵܐܝܼܬ
whichever	ܐܲܝܢܵܐ	perpetual	ܐܲܡܝܼܢܵܐ
daylight, day	ܐܝܼܡܵܡܵܐ	perpetuity	ܐܲܡܝܼܢܘܼܬ݂ܵܐ
when	ܐܸܡܲܬ݂	prince	ܐܸܡܝܼܪܵܐ
yes	ܐܹܝܢ	say, tell	ܐܵܡܹܪ، ܐܡܝܼܪܵܐ
praise, honor, dignity	ܐܝܼܩܵܪܵܐ	if	ܐܸܢ
May	ܐܝܼܵܪ	I	ܐܵܢܵܐ
there is/are	ܐܝܼܬ	man, human being	ܐܢܵܫܵܐ
you (m, f)	ܐܲܢܬ، ܐܲܢܬܝ	women	ܐܸܢܫܹܐ
essence, being	ܐܝܼܬܘܼܬ݂ܵܐ	humanity	ܐܢܵܫܘܼܬ݂ܵܐ
Divine being, being	ܐܝܼܬܝܵܐ	humane	ܐܢܵܫܵܝܵܐ
here	ܐܵܟ݂ܵܐ، ܗܵܟ݂ܵܐ	prodigal	ܐܵܣܘܿܛܵܐ
eat, consume	ܐܵܟܹܠ، ܐܝܼܟܼܠܵܐ	debauchery	ܐܵܣܘܿܛܘܼܬ݂ܵܐ
you (pl)	ܐܲܚܬܘܿܢ	physician	ܐܵܣܝܵܐ
		medicine	ܐܵܣܝܘܼܬ݂ܵܐ

prisoner	ܐܒܝܼܣܐ	archdeacon	ܐܪܟܝܕܝܩܢܐ
slavery	ܐܒܝܕܘܬܐ	chief	ܐܪܟܘܢܐ
ascend	ܐܣܩ، ܐܣܩ	pomegranate	ܐܪܡܢܐ
bind, tie	ܐܣܪ، ܐܣܪ	widowhood	ܐܪܡܠܘܬܐ
conjunction	ܐܣܪܐ	widow	ܐܪܡܠܬܐ
chai glass	ܐܣܬܟܢ	widower	ܐܪܡܠܐ
also	ܐܦ	land, earth, ground	ܐܪܥܐ
although	ܐܦܢ	earthly	ܐܪܥܢܝܐ
not even	ܐܦܠܐ	seventeen	ܐܫܬܥܣܪ
bishop	ܐܦܣܩܦܐ	six	ܐܫܬܐ
manuscript	ܐܦܪܣܐ	sole	ܐܫܬܐ ܕܣܢܐ
foot, leg	ܐܩܠܐ	bottom	ܐܫܬܐ ܕܣܝܒ
four	ܐܪܒܥܐ	sixty	ܐܫܬܝܢ
Wednesday	ܐܪܒܥܒܫܒܐ	sixteen	ܐܫܬܥܣܪ
forty	ܐܪܒܥܝܢ	come	ܐܬܐ، ܐܬܐ
fourteen	ܐܪܒܥܣܪ	furnace	ܐܬܘܢܐ
purple	ܐܪܓܘܢܐ	letter	ܐܬܘܬܐ
cedar	ܐܪܙܐ	land, country	ܐܬܪܐ
mystery, Mass, sacrament	ܐܪܙܐ	territorial	ܐܬܪܢܐ
cheap	ܐܪܙܢ		ܒ
guest	ܐܪܚܐ	in	ܒـ
feast	ܐܪܚܣܡܐ	well	ܒܐܪܐ
grinding mill	ܐܪܚܝܐ	father	ܒܒܐ
lion	ܐܪܝܐ	step father	ܒܒܘܢܐ
lioness	ܐܪܝܣܡܐ	pupil of the eye	ܒܒܬܐ

103

English	Chaldean	English	Chaldean
fatherhood	ܬܚܡܗܐ	meal	ܠܘܼܥܠܐ
Babylon	ܒܒܠ	pebble	ܚܨܨܐ
together	ܒܚܕܝܘ	together	ܒܚܕܝܘ
in, into	ܒܓܘ	search	ܒܨܬ، ܒܨܬܐ
within	ܒܓܘ	stop, eradicate	ܒܛܠ، ܒܛܠܐ
alone	ܒܠܚܘܕ	cease, be idle	ܒܛܠ، ܒܛܠܐ
garment	ܒܘܫܐ	conceive	ܒܛܢ، ܒܛܢܐ
light	ܒܗܪܐ	idle	ܒܛܝܠܐ
luminous	ܒܗܘܪܐ	idleness	ܒܛܝܠܘܬܐ
be ashamed	ܒܗܬ، ܒܗܬܐ	conceived	ܒܛܝܢܐ
shame	ܒܗܬܐ	pregnancy	ܒܛܢܬܐ
examination	ܒܘܚܪܢܐ	forehead	ܒܝܬ ܥܝܢܐ
firstborn	ܒܘܟܪܐ	through, by means of	ܒܝܕ
birthright	ܒܘܟܪܘܬܐ	spill	ܒܝܒ، ܒܢܒܐ
nightingale	ܒܘܠܒܘܠܐ	pulpit	ܒܝܡ
babbling	ܒܘܠܒܠܐ	between, among	ܒܝܢ
pleasure	ܒܘܣܡܐ	between, among	ܒܝܢܬ
herd	ܒܘܩܪܐ	evil	ܒܝܫܐ
question	ܒܘܩܪܐ	wickedness	ܒܝܫܘܬܐ
fool	ܒܘܪܐ	evil	ܒܝܫܬܐ
tower	ܒܘܪܓܐ	house, family	ܒܝܬܐ
screw	ܒܘܪܓܐ	home	ܒܝܬ ܕܝܪܐ
knee	ܒܘܪܟܐ	prison	ܒܝܬ ܐܣܝܪܐ
wedding	ܒܘܪܟܐ	hostelry	ܒܝܬ ܒܘܬܐ
blessing	ܒܘܪܟܬܐ	archive	ܒܝܬ ܐܪܟܐ

English	Chaldean	English	Chaldean
refuge asylum	ܒܝܬ ܓܘܣܐ	alone	ܒܠܚܘܕܘܗܝ
house treasury	ܒܝܬ ܓܙܐ	busy, worn out	ܒܠܝܼܠܐ
wedding house	ܒܝܬ ܓܢܘܢܐ	busy	ܒܠܒܠܐ
school	ܒܝܬ ܘܕܪܐ	billion	ܒܠܝܘܢ
judgment house	ܒܝܬ ܕܝܢܐ	perhaps	ܒܠܚܘܕ
Epiphany Season	ܒܝܬ ܕܢܚܐ	swallow	ܒܠܥ، ܒܠܥ
appointed place	ܒܝܬ ܘܥܕܐ	build	ܒܢܐ، ܒܢܐ
Christmas	ܒܝܬ ܝܠܕܐ	builder	ܒܢܝܐ
library	ܒܝܬ ܟܬܒܐ	people, men	ܒܢܝܢܫܐ
water closet	ܒܝܬ ܡܝܐ	bank	ܒܢܟܐ
sanctuary	ܒܝܬ ܡܩܕܫܐ	then; therefore	ܒܤ
hospital	ܒܝܬ ܡܪܥܐ	enough	ܒܤܐ
baptistery	ܒܝܬ ܥܡܕܐ	pleasant	ܒܤܝܡܐ
family	ܒܝܬܘܬܐ	agreeably	ܒܤܝܡܐܝܬ
familiar	ܒܝܬܝܐ	pleasantness	ܒܤܝܡܘܬܐ
Beth Nahreyn, Mesopotamia	ܒܝܬܢܗܪܝܢ	be agreeable, heal	ܒܤܡ، ܒܤܡ
cry	ܒܟܐ، ܒܟܐ	incense	ܒܤܡܐ
woman, wife	ܒܟܬܐ	nail	ܒܤܡܪܐ
little woman	ܒܟܬܘܢܐ	flesh, meat	ܒܤܪܐ
effeminate	ܒܟܬܢܐ	gums	ܒܤܪܐ ܘܟܟܐ
front	ܒܠܕ	fleshy, carnal	ܒܤܪܢܐ
without	ܒܠܐ	familiarity	ܒܤܝܡܘܬܐ
decay	ܒܠܐ، ܒܠܐ	garden	ܒܤܬܢܐ
throat	ܒܠܥܘܡܐ	egg	ܒܥܬܐ، ܒܥܐ
glutton	ܒܠܥܘܡܢܐ	want	ܒܥܐ، ܒܥܐ

petition	ܒܥܘܬܐ
beloved	ܒܥܝܐ
coal	ܒܨܐ
lacking	ܒܨܝܪܐ
onion	ܒܨܠܐ
gnat, mosquito	ܒܩܐ
bubble	ܒܩܒܩ، ܒܩܒܘܩܐ
large bean	ܒܩܠܠܐ
ask	ܒܩܪ، ܒܩܘܪܐ
inquiry	ܒܩܪܬܐ
son of	ܒܪ
countryman	ܒܪ ܐܬܪܐ
create	ܒܪܐ، ܒܪܝܐ
spill, scatter, disperse	ܒܪܒܙ، ܒܪܒܘܙܐ
barbarian	ܒܪܒܪܝܐ
hail	ܒܪܕܐ
Creator	ܒܪܘܝܐ
son/boy	ܒܪܘܢܐ
seed, descendant	ܒܪܙܪܥܐ
brother in law	ܒܪܚܡܝܐ
sister in law	ܒܪܚܡܝܬܐ
outside of	ܒܪܝ ܡܢ
created	ܒܪܝܐ
outer	ܒܪܝܐ
wilderness	ܒܪܝܐ
blessed	ܒܪܝܟܐ
creation	ܒܪܝܬܐ
kneel	ܒܪܟ، ܒܪܟܐ
barrel	ܒܪܡܝܠܐ
man	ܒܪܢܫܐ
lightening	ܒܪܩܐ
opposite	ܒܪܩܘܒܠ
adversary	ܒܪܩܘܒܠܢܐ
in the beginning	ܒܪܫܝܬ
namesake	ܒܪܫܡܐ
girl, daughter	ܒܪܬܐ
echo	ܒܪܬܩܠܐ
more	ܒܫ
more than; especially	ܒܫ ܚܕܕ
better	ܒܫ ܛܒ
cooked	ܒܫܝܠܐ
melon	ܒܫܝܠܐ
welcome	ܒܫܝܢܐ
cook	ܒܫܠ، ܒܫܘܠܐ
virgin	ܒܬܘܠܐ
virginity	ܒܬܘܠܘܬܐ
after, behind	ܒܬܪ
	ܓ
tire	ܓܘܐ، ܓܘܢܐ
tired, weary	ܓܘܝܐ

stir ܓ̰ܘܓ̰، ܓ̰ܘܓ̰ܓ̰ܐ
group ܓ̰ܘܩܐ
clothes ܓ̰ܘܠܠܐ
adolescent ܓ̰ܘܚܠܐ
young man ܓ̰ܘܚܠܘܢܐ
adolescence ܓ̰ܘܚܠܘܬܐ
temptation ܓ̰ܘܪܒܐ
island ܓ̰ܘܙܪܬܐ
rust ܓ̰ܢܓ̰ܪܐ
flow ܓ̰ܪܐ، ܓ̰ܪܝܐ
wound ܓ̰ܪܚ، ܓ̰ܪܚܐ
cut ܓ̰ܪܚܐ
slip ܓ̰ܪܛ، ܓ̰ܪܛܐ
flow ܓ̰ܪܝܢܬܐ
arrow ܓ̰ܐܪܐ
side ܓܒܐ
beg ܓܒܐ، ܓܒܝܐ
nearby ܓܒܝ
beggar ܓܒܝܐ
beggarliness ܓܒܝܘܬܐ
brow ܓܒܝܢܐ
sad ܓܒܝܢܐ
mix ܓܒܠ، ܓܒܠܐ
vomit ܓܒܠܐ ܓܒܐ
formation ܓܒܠܬܐ

man, husband ܓܒܪܐ
marry ܓܒܪ، ܓܒܪܐ
little man ܓܒܪܘܢܐ
Golgotha ܓܓܘܠܬܐ
braided ܓܕܝܠܐ
happened ܓܕܫܐ
abbreviation ܓܕܡܬܐ
blaspheme ܓܕܦ، ܓܕܘܦܐ
happen ܓܕܫ، ܓܕܫܐ
accident, happening ܓܕܫܐ
accidental ܓܕܫܢܝܐ
string, yarn ܓܕܕܐ
weaver ܓܕܠܢܐ
abbreviate ܓܕܡ، ܓܕܡܐ
time ܓܗܐ
inclination ܓܗܝܬܐ
in, into ܓܘ
inside ܓܘܐ
inwardly ܓܘܐܝܬ
pit ܓܘܒܐ
wall ܓܘܕܐ
blasphemy ܓܘܕܦܐ
walnut ܓܘܙܐ
interior ܓܘܝܐ
slave, servant ܓܘܠܡܐ

slavery	ܓܘܠܡܘܬܐ
wing	ܓܘܠܦܐ
camel	ܓܘܡܠܐ
handful	ܓܘܡܙܐ
hole	ܓܘܡܬܐ
universally, generally	ܓܘܢܝܐܝܬ
universal	ܓܘܢܝܐ
cheese	ܓܘܦܬܐ
whelp; puppy	ܓܘܪܝܐ
baptismal font	ܓܘܪܢܐ
flesh, substance	ܓܘܫܡܐ
concrete	ܓܘܫܡܢܝܐ
treasury	ܓܙܐ
circumcision	ܓܘܙܪܬܐ
poor thing	ܓܘܝܠܘ، ܓܝܘܝܠܗ
laugh	ܓܚܟ، ܓܚܟܐ
laughter	ܓܝܚܟܐ
circle	ܓܝܓܠܐ
hell	ܓܝܗܢܐ
carrot	ܓܝܙܪܐ
soul	ܓܝܢܐ
robber	ܓܝܣܐ
adulter	ܓܝܪܐ
adulteress	ܓܝܪܬܐ
grass, hay	ܓܠܐ
reveal	ܓܠܐ، ܓܠܝܐ
conquer	ܓܠܒ، ܓܠܒܐ
conquest	ܓܠܒܘܬܐ
skin, hide	ܓܠܕܐ
mistake	ܓܠܛܐ
err	ܓܠܛ، ܓܠܛܐ
valley	ܓܠܠܬܐ
ice	ܓܠܝܕܐ
revelation	ܓܠܝܢܐ
lock	ܓܠܡ، ܓܠܡܐ
ember	ܓܡܘܪܬܐ
ship, boat	ܓܡܝܬܐ
be completed, perfected	ܓܡܪ، ܓܡܪܐ
incline	ܓܢܐ، ܓܢܝܐ
steal	ܓܢܒ، ܓܢܒܐ
thief	ܓܢܒܐ
hero, warrior	ܓܢܒܪܐ
heroism	ܓܢܒܪܘܬܐ
fault	ܓܢܘܬܐ
wedding house	ܓܢܘܢܐ
stolen	ܓܢܝܒܐ
race, kind	ܓܢܣܐ
generic	ܓܢܣܢܝܐ
garden	ܓܢܬܐ

cave ܓܘܦܬܐ

leprosy ܓܪܒܐ

socks ܓܪ̈ܒܐ

north ܓܪܒܝܐ

northern ܓܪܒܝܝܐ

leper ܓܪܒܢܐ

must ܓܪܓ

thunder ܓܪܓܡ، ܓܪܓܘܡܐ

thunder ܓܪܓܡܬܐ

strip off ܓܪܕ، ܓܪܕܐ

axle, rolling pin ܓܪܘܡܐ

rolling pin ܓܪܘܡܐ

garage ܓܪܐܓ̰

ivory ܓܪܡ ܦܝܠܐ

bone ܓܪܡܐ

bony ܓܪܡܢܐ

grind ܓܪܣ، ܓܪܣܐ

shave ܓܪܥ، ܓܪܥܐ

barber ܓܪܥܐ

shovel ܓܪܦ، ܓܪܦܐ

pull ܓܪܫ، ܓܪܫܐ

foolish ܓܫܝܡ

bridge ܓܫܪܐ

spying ܓܫܫ، ܓܫܘܫܐ

ܕ

of; so that ܕ-

wolf ܕܐܒܐ

prolong ܕܐܡ، ܕܝܡܐ

judge ܕܐܢ، ܕܝܢܐ

grind ܕܐܩ، ܕܝܩܐ

press, trample ܕܐܫ، ܕܝܫܐ

bear ܕܒܐ

wasp ܕܒܘܪܐ

sacrifice ܕܒܚ، ܕܒܚܐ

sacrifice ܕܒܚܐ

livelihood ܕܒܪܐ

bee ܕܒܫܐ

honey ܕܒܫܐ

lie ܕܓܠ، ܕܓܠܘܬܐ

liar ܕܓܠܐ

dear kid ܕܕܐ

fly ܕܕܘܐ

now ܕܗܐ

gold ܕܗܒܐ

golden ܕܗܒܢܐ

drum ܕܗܘܠܐ

oily ܕܗܝܢܐ

oil ܕܗܢܐ

deed ܕܘܒܪܐ

English	Chaldean	English	Chaldean
lie; falsehood	ܕܘܓܠܬܐ	debtor	ܕܝܢܢܐ
button	ܕܘܓܡܬܐ	coin	ܕܝܢܪܐ
David	ܕܘܝܕ	very small	ܕܝܣܡܢܐ
Psalter	ܕܘܝܕܐ	monastery	ܕܝܪܐ
place	ܕܘܟܐ، ܕܘܟܬܐ	monk	ܕܝܪܝܐ
memorial	ܕܘܟܪܢܐ	step on	ܕܝܫ، ܕܝܫܐ
closet, cupboard	ܕܘܠܒܐ	clean	ܕܟܐ، ܕܟܝܐ
stuffed vine-leaves	ܕܘܠܡܐ	masculine	ܕܟܪܢܝܐ
country	ܕܘܠܬܐ	without	ܕܠܐ
resemblance	ܕܘܡܝܐ	little	ܕܠܝܠܐ
world	ܕܘܢܝܐ	produce; fruit	ܕܠܝܬܐ
branch	ܕܘܣܬܐ	leak	ܕܠܩ، ܕܠܩܐ
age	ܕܘܪܐ	blood	ܕܡܐ
investigation	ܕܘܪܫܐ	resemble	ܕܡܐ، ܕܡܝܐ
dust	ܕܒܝܢܐ	drum	ܕܡܟܐ
bush	ܕܣܟܐ	likeness	ܕܡܘܬܐ
demon	ܕܝܘܐ	sleep	ܕܡܟ، ܕܡܟܐ
insane, demoniac	ܕܝܘܢܐ	bloody	ܕܡܢܐ
sitting room	ܕܝܘܢܣܢܐ	tear	ܕܡܥܬܐ
as, how	ܕܝܟ	ice cream	ܕܢܕܘܡܐ
rooster	ܕܝܟܐ	tail	ܕܢܒܐ
belonging to	ܕܝܠ	Epiphany	ܕܢܚܐ
debt	ܕܝܢܐ	card	ܕܗܡܐ
judge	ܕܝܢܐ	kettle	ܕܗܒܝܬܐ
judgment	ܕܝܢܐ	permission	ܕܗܘܬ

110

English	Chaldean	English	Chaldean
pot	ܕܘܕܝܬܐ	courtyard	ܕܪܬܐ
turn off	ܕܥܟ، ܕܥܟܐ	sleepwear	ܕܡܟܬܐ
see	ܕܝܠ، ܕܝܠܐ	enemy	ܕܥܡܝ
sweat	ܕܥܝ، ܕܥܝܐ	enmity	ܕܥܡܝܢܘܬܐ
sweat	ܕܥܬܐ	plain	ܕܫܬܐ
board	ܕܦܐ	establish	ܕܬܐ، ܕܬܗ
side	ܕܦܢܐ	ܗ	
tiny	ܕܥܝܩܬܐ	behold	ܗܐ
Tigris	ܕܩܠܬ	give (imperative)	ܗܒ
beard	ܕܩܢܐ	persecute	ܗܓܠܝ، ܗܓܘܦܠܬܐ
age	ܕܩܢܐ	attack	ܗܓܡ، ܗܓܡܬܐ
degree	ܕܪܓܐ	tonight	ܗܕ ܠܝܠܐ
cradle	ܕܪܓܘܫܬܐ	threaten	ܗܕܕ، ܗܕܘܕܬܐ
of degree, rank	ܕܪܓܝܐ	gently	ܗܕܝ
complain	ܕܕܢܡ، ܕܕܘܢܡܘ	member, limb	ܗܕܡܐ
complaint	ܕܕܢܡܬܐ	membership	ܗܕܡܘܬܐ
dervish	ܕܪܘܝܫ	this	ܗܕ
disputant	ܕܪܘܫܬܐ	thus	ܗܕܝܟ
danger	ܕܪܩ	this	ܗܕܒ
medicine	ܕܪܡܢܐ	he	ܗܘ
study	ܕܪܫ، ܕܪܫܐ	be, be born	ܗܘܐ، ܗܘܢܐ
arm	ܕܪܥܐ	discipline	ܗܘܟܢܐ
against	ܕܩܘܒܠ	mind	ܗܘܢܐ
opposed	ܕܩܘܒܠܢܝܐ	intellectual, smart	ܗܘܢܢܐ
study	ܕܪܫ، ܕܪܫܬܐ		

111

sub deacon	ܗܘܦܕܝܩܢܐ
jar	ܗܘܕܐ
wail, cry for help	ܗܘܪ
abyss	ܗܘܬܐ
then; at the time	ܗܝܕܝܟ
during	ܗܝܕܟܐ
come	ܗܝܐ
temple, nave	ܗܝܟܠܐ
cardamom	ܗܝܠ
faith	ܗܝܡܢܘܬܐ
until	ܗܠ
cheer	ܗܠܗܠ، ܗܠܗܘܠܐ
perish	ܗܠܟ، ܗܠܟܬܐ
halleluiah	ܗܠܠܘܝܐ
even if	ܗܡ
sweet	ܗܢܝܐ
only	ܗܪ
heretical	ܗܪܛܝܩܐ
heresy	ܗܪܣܝܣ
spirited	ܗܪܥܐ
still, yet	ܗܫ
cautious	ܗܫܝܪ
	ܘ
and	ܘ-
veil	ܘܠܐ
ambassador	ܘܦܕܐ
cartridge	ܘܫܟܐ
beast	ܘܚܫܐ
alas	ܘܝ
until	ܘܥܠ
promise	ܘܥܕ، ܘܥܕܬܐ
promise	ܘܥܕܐ
rag	ܘܨܠܐ
flower, rose	ܘܪܕܐ
rosary	ܘܪܕܝܬܐ
root, vein	ܘܪܝܕܐ
paper	ܘܪܩܐ
	ܙ
buy	ܙܒܢ، ܙܒܢܐ
time, season	ܙܒܢܐ
seasonable	ܙܒܢܢܝܐ
bell	ܙܓܐ
fear	ܙܕܘܥܬܐ
righteous, just	ܙܕܝܩܐ
justly	ܙܕܝܩܐܝܬ
fear	ܙܝܥ، ܙܝܥܐ
alms	ܙܕܩܬܐ
dairy	ܙܗܘܐ
ray of light	ܙܗܪܝܪܐ

pair, double	ܙܘܓܐ
extra	ܙܘܝܕܐ
caution, explanation	ܙܘܗܪܐ
marriage, union	ܙܘܘܓܐ
coin, money	ܙܘܙܐ
religious procession	ܙܘܝܚܐ
song, chant	ܙܘܡܪܐ
movement, vowel, earthquake	ܙܘܥܐ
hyssop	ܙܘܦܐ
pipe	ܙܘܪܢܐ
be bold	ܙܝܣܡ، ܙܣܡܐ
bold	ܙܣܡܐ
armor	ܙܝܢܐ
olive	ܙܝܬܐ
victory	ܙܟܘܬܐ
victorious	ܙܟܝܐ
small fragment	ܙܠܝܡܐ
song	ܙܡܘܪܬܐ
sung	ܙܡܝܪܐ
sing	ܙܡܪ، ܙܡܪܐ
singer	ܙܡܪܐ
fornicate	ܙܢܐ، ܙܢܝܐ
black bird	ܙܢܘܪܐ
fornicator	ܙܢܝܐ

fornication	ܙܢܝܘܬܐ
prostitute	ܙܢܝܬܐ
small	ܙܥܘܪܐ
small	ܙܥܘܪܐ
cross	ܙܩܝܦܐ
weave	ܙܩܪ، ܙܩܪܐ
weaver	ܙܩܪܐ
strong	ܙܪܝܙܐ
sow	ܙܪܥ، ܙܪܥܐ
seed	ܙܪܥܐ
sower	ܙܪܥܐ
dawn	ܙܪܩ، ܙܪܩܐ
blue	ܙܪܩܐ
	ܚ
free	ܚܐܪܐ
freedom	ܚܐܪܘܬܐ
dearest	ܚܒܒܐ
apple	ܚܒܘܫܐ
imprisonment	ܚܒܘܫܝܐ
storm	ܚܒܛܐ
mix	ܚܒܛ، ܚܒܛܐ
beloved	ܚܒܝܒܐ
rope	ܚܒܠܐ
take prisoner	ܚܒܫ، ܚܒܫܐ
friend	ܚܒܪܐ

enclose	ܚܒܫ، ܚܒܫܐ
dancing chorus	ܚܓܐ
one	ܚܕ
Sunday	ܚܕܒܫܒܐ
traveler	ܚܕܘܪܐ
eleven	ܚܕܥܣܪ
around	ܚܕܪܘܢܝ
New Testament	ܚܕܬܐ
one another	ܚܕܕܐ
gladness	ܚܕܘܬܐ
unity	ܚܕܝܘܬܐ
ready	ܚܕܝܪܐ
some	ܚܕܟܡܐ
singular	ܚܕܢܝܐ
wrap	ܚܕܟ، ܚܕܟܐ
travel, encircle	ܚܕܪ، ܚܕܪܐ
debt, trespass	ܚܘܒܐ
love	ܚܘܒܐ
loving	ܚܘܒܢܐ
Breviary	ܚܘܕܪܐ
renewal; dedication	ܚܘܕܬܐ
around	ܚܘܕܪܢܝ
snake	ܚܘܘܐ
would that...	ܚܘܝܒ ܕ
peach	ܚܘܚܐ
stick, staff, rod	ܚܘܛܪܐ
dream	ܚܘܠܡܐ
health	ܚܘܠܡܢܐ
absolution	ܚܘܣܝܐ
loss, want	ܚܘܣܪܢܐ
jar	ܚܘܨܐ
whiten	ܚܘܪ، ܚܘܪܐ
white	ܚܘܪܐ
white beard, elder	ܚܘܪܕܩܢܐ
thought, idea	ܚܘܫܒܐ
excuse	ܚܘܫܒܬܐ
under	ܚܘܬ
below	ܚܘܬܝ
ending	ܚܘܬܡܐ
see	ܚܙܐ، ܚܙܝܐ
vision	ܚܙܘܐ
pig	ܚܙܝܪܐ
seer	ܚܙܝܐ
June	ܚܙܝܪܢ
relative	ܚܝܡܐ
attend	ܚܛܪ، ܚܛܪܐ
wheat	ܚܛܐ
sin	ܚܛܐ، ܚܛܝܐ
ravenous	ܚܛܘܦܐ
sinner	ܚܛܝܐ

English	Chaldean	English	Chaldean
corn of wheat	ܚܛܝܬܐ	wedding feast	ܡܫܬܘܬܐ
sin	ܚܛܝܬܐ	milk	ܚܠܒܐ
seize	ܚܛܦ، ܚܛܦܐ	permitted	ܚܠܠ
life	ܚܝܐ	dream	ܚܠܡ، ܚܠܡܐ
live	ܚܝܐ، ܚܝܐ	instead of	ܚܠܦ
sew	ܚܝܛ، ܚܝܛܐ	pronoun	ܚܠܦܫܡܐ
sewer	ܚܝܛܐ	salvation	ܚܠܝ
scratch	ܚܟܟ، ܚܟܟܐ	weak	ܚܠܫܐ
strength, power	ܚܝܠܐ	maternal aunt	ܚܠܬܐ
powerful	ܚܝܠܢܐ	hot (weather)	ܚܡܐ
mighty	ܚܝܠܬܢܐ	keep	ܚܡܠ، ܚܡܠܐ
warm	ܚܡܝܡܐ، ܚܡܡ	sour	ܚܡܘܥܐ
tent	ܚܡܠܐ	hot, warm	ܚܡܝܡܐ
have pity	ܚܢܢ، ܚܢܢܐ	leaven	ܚܡܝܪܐ
bathe	ܚܦܦ، ܚܦܐ	fifth	ܚܡܝܫܐ
look	ܚܙܐ، ܚܙܝܐ	stop	ܚܡܠ، ܚܡܠܐ
wild cucumber	ܚܙܘܪܐ	standing	ܚܡܠܐ
doctor	ܚܟܝܡܐ، ܐܣܝܐ	bathroom	ܚܡܡ
wise	ܚܟܝܡܐ	sour	ܚܡܥܐ، ܚܡܝܥ
wisdom	ܚܟܡܬܐ	donkey	ܚܡܪܐ
maternal uncle	ܚܠܐ	wine	ܚܡܪܐ
vinegar	ܚܠܐ	she-donkey	ܚܡܪܬܐ
sweeten	ܚܠܐ، ܚܠܐ	five	ܚܡܫܐ
yogurt	ܚܠܒܐ	Thursday	ܚܡܫܒܫܒܐ
sweet, beautiful	ܚܠܘܐ	fifty	ܚܡܫܝ

115

fifteen	ܚܡܫܬܥܣܪܐ
anger	ܚܡܬܐ
maiden	ܚܡܬܐ
mother-in-law	ܚܡܬܐ
dagger	ܚܢܓܪܐ
embalm	ܚܢܛ، ܚܢܛܐ
merciful	ܚܢܢܐ
pity	ܚܢܢܐ
heathen	ܚܢܦܐ
strangle	ܚܢܩ، ܚܢܩܐ
reckon	ܚܫܒ، ܚܫܒܐ
envy	ܚܣܕ، ܚܣܕܐ
lacking	ܚܣܝܪܐ
lose	ܚܣܪ، ܚܣܪܐ
barefoot	ܚܦܝܢܐ
hug	ܚܦܩ، ܚܦܩܐ
dig	ܚܦܪ، ܚܦܪܐ
what a pity!	ܚܝܦ
back	ܚܨܐ
reap	ܚܨܕ، ܚܨܕܐ
reaper	ܚܨܘܕܐ
justice	ܚܩ
truth	ܚܩܘܬܐ
field	ܚܩܠܐ
destroy	ܚܪܒ، ܚܪܒܐ
war	ܚܪܒܐ
dumb	ܚܪܫܐ
sharpness	ܚܪܦܐ
free	ܚܪܪ، ܚܪܘܪܐ
dumb, without understanding	ܚܪܫܐ
wizard	ܚܪܫܐ
end	ܚܪܬܐ
sorrow	ܚܫܐ
think	ܚܫܒ، ܚܫܒܐ
account, reckoning	ܚܘܫܒܢܐ
fit, useful	ܚܫܚ
be useful	ܚܫܚ، ܚܫܚܐ
darken	ܚܫܟ، ܚܫܟܐ
sorrowful	ܚܫܝܫܐ
sister	ܚܬܐ
lady	ܚܬܘܢ
lower	ܚܬܝܐ
seal, finish	ܚܬܡ، ܚܬܡܐ
bridegroom	ܚܬܢܐ

ܛ

good	ܛܒܐ
table	ܛܒܠܝܬܐ
dust	ܛܘܙ
mountain	ܛܘܪܐ
value	ܛܝܡܐ

wander	ܛܥܐ، ܛܥܝܐ
oppression	ܛܠܘܡܝܐ
for me	ܛܠܝ
oppress	ܛܠܡ، ܛܠܡܐ
tomato	ܛܡܛܐ
taste	ܛܥܡ، ܛܥܡܐ
flavor	ܛܥܡܐ
belt	ܛܣܡܐ
strap	ܛܣܡܐ
obey	ܛܐܥ، ܛܐܥܐ
murmor	ܛܪܛܡ، ܛܪܛܘܡܐ
good	ܛܒܐ
report	ܛܒܐ
August	ܛܒܚ
crush	ܛܒܚ، ܛܒܚܐ
print	ܛܒܥ، ܛܒܥܐ
benefit	ܛܒܬܐ
roast	ܛܘܐ، ܛܘܝܐ
bead	ܛܘܒܬܐ
happy, blessed	ܛܘܒܢܐ
race, tribe	ܛܘܗܡܐ
type; pattern	ܛܘܦܣܐ
flood	ܛܘܦܢܐ
fingernail	ܛܘܦܪܐ
mountain	ܛܘܪܐ
mountainous	ܛܘܪܢܐ
grace	ܛܝܒܘܬܐ
value	ܛܝܡܐ
precious	ܛܝܡܢܐ
mud, clay	ܛܝܢܐ
bird	ܛܝܪܐ
order	ܛܟܣܐ
shade	ܛܠܐ
espousal	ܛܠܝܒܘܬܐ
suitor	ܛܠܘܒܐ
betrothed woman	ܛܠܝܒܬܐ
little girl	ܛܠܝܬܐ
shadow	ܛܠܠܝܬܐ
bury	ܛܡܪ، ܛܡܪܐ
dip	ܛܡܫ، ܛܡܫܐ
unclean	ܛܡܐܐ
carry	ܛܥܢ، ܛܥܢܐ
fold	ܛܥܦ، ܛܥܦܐ
stick	ܛܦܐ، ܛܦܢܐ
nail, claw	ܛܦܪܐ
drive away	ܛܪܕ، ܛܪܕܐ
strike	ܛܪܦ، ܛܪܦܐ
leaf	ܛܪܦܐ
leafy	ܛܪܦܢܐ

English	Chaldean	English	Chaldean
become fat	ܒܠܛܝ، ܒܠܛܝܐ	sea	ܝܡܐ
privacy; secrecy	ܟܣܝܐ	swear an oath	ܝܡܝ، ܝܡܝܐ
	ܡ	motherhood	ܝܡܘܬܐ
or	ܝܢ، ܝܢ	right, right hand	ܝܡܝܢܐ، ܝܡܝܢ
raisin	ܝܒܫܬܐ	right-handed	ܝܡܝܢܝܐ
dry	ܝܒܝܫ، ܝܒܝܫܐ	lake	ܝܡܬܐ
dry land	ܝܒܫܬܐ	bake	ܝܦܐ، ܝܦܢܐ
knower	ܝܕܘܥܐ	burn	ܝܩܕ، ܝܩܕܐ
know	ܝܕܥ، ܝܕܥܐ	heavy	ܝܩܘܪܐ
give	ܝܗܒܠ، ܝܗܒ	honored	ܝܩܝܪܐ
learning	ܝܘܠܦܢܐ	make heave	ܝܩܪ، ܝܩܪܐ
day	ܝܘܡܐ	green	ܝܘܪܩܐ
dove	ܝܘܢܐ	heir	ܝܪܘܬܐ
weight, load	ܝܘܩܪܐ	month	ܝܪܚܐ
inheritance	ܝܘܪܬܢܐ	long	ܝܪܝܟܐ
only begotten	ܝܚܝܕܝܐ	extend	ܝܪܟ، ܝܪܟܐ
only begotten	ܝܚܝܕܐ	length	ܝܪܟܐ
Birth, Nativity	ܝܠܕܐ	inherit	ܝܪܬ، ܝܪܬܐ
boy	ܝܠܕܐ	inheritance	ܝܪܬܘܬܐ
little boy	ܝܠܕܘܢܐ	Jesus	ܝܫܘܥ
bear children	ܝܠܕ، ܝܠܕܐ	sit	ܝܬܒ، ܝܬܒܐ
boy	ܝܠܘܕܐ	orphan	ܝܬܘܡܐ
father	ܝܠܘܕܐ		ܟ
learn	ܝܠܦ، ܝܠܦܐ	like	ܟ-
mother	ܝܡܐ	tea	ܟܐܝ

118

nothing, no ܟ̰ܘ
wilderness ܟ̰ܘܿܠ
nothing ܟ̰ܘܡܸܢܕܝ
weapon, tool ܟ̰ܟ̰ܐ
serving spoon ܟ̰ܡܟ̰ܐ
fork ܟ̰ܢܓܠ
handful ܟ̰ܦܐ
left ܟ̰ܦ̈ܐ
dirty ܟ̰ܦܠ
sheet ܟ̰ܪܟ̰ܘ
upright, just ܟܐܢܐ
justly ܟܐܢܐܝܬ
cup ܟܣܐ
stone, rock ܟܐܦܐ
stony ܟܐܦܢܐ
great, much ܟܒܝܪܐ
perhaps ܟܒܪܢܐ
like, as ܟܕܝܠܝܕ
serve ܟܕܡ، ܟܕܡܐ
man-servant ܟܕܡܐ
maid-servant ܟܕܡܬܐ
priest ܟܗܢܐ
when ܟܘܕ
spicy ܟܘܝܐ
star ܟܘܟܒܐ

all ܟܘܠ، ܟܘܿܠ، ܟܠ
Crowning of the Church ܟܘܠܠ ܥܕܬܐ
Sanctification of the Church ܟܘܠܠ ܥܕܬܐ
crowning ܟܘܠܠܐ
black ܟܘܡܐ
high priest ܟܘܡܪܐ
hair ܟܘܣܐ
hat ܟܘܣܝܬܐ
lowly ܟܘܦܐ
blind ܟܘܪܐ
illness ܟܘܪܗܢܐ
shroud ܟܘܪܟܐ
seat, chair ܟܘܪܣܝܐ
supplication ܟܘܫܦܐ
shirt, tunic ܟܘܬܝܢܐ
blot ܟܘܬܡܐ
measure ܟܝܠ، ܟܝܠܐ
blacken ܟܝܡ، ܟܝܡܐ
nature ܟܝܢܐ
naturally ܟܝܢܐܝܬ
bag ܟܝܣܐ
bend down ܟܝܦ، ܟܝܦܐ
tooth ܟܟܐ
stop ܟܠܐ، ܟܠܝܐ

dog	ܟܲܠܒܵܐ
Chaldean	ܟܲܠܕܵܝܵܐ
daily	ܟܠܝܘܡ
crown	ܟܠܝܠܵܐ
sandals	ܟܲܠܟܹ̈ܐ
entirely	ܟܠܵܢܵܝܗ
very	ܟܠܝܼܫ
bride	ܟܲܠܬܵܐ
how much, how many	ܟܡܵܐ
mouth	ܟܹܡܵܐ
quantity	ܟܡܝܘܼܬܵܐ
fade	ܟܡܹܫ، ܟܡܵܫܵܐ
pear	ܟܡܸܬܪܵܐ
December	ܟܵܢܘܿܢ ܐ
January	ܟܵܢܘܿܢ ܒ
gathering	ܟܢܘܼܫܝܵܐ
collective	ܟܢܘܼܫܝܵܝܵܐ
wing	ܟܢܦܵܐ
harp	ܟܢܵܪܵܐ
sweep	ܟܢܸܫ، ܟܢܵܫܵܐ
assembly	ܟܢܫܵܐ
cup	ܟܣܵܐ
bedspread	ܟܣܘܼܝܵܐ
lazy	ܟܣܠܵܢ
wallet	ܟܸܣܬܵܐ

ungodly, unbelieving	ܟܵܦܘܼܪܵܐ
hungry	ܟܦܝܼܢܵܐ
hunger	ܟܦܸܢ، ܟܦܵܢܵܐ
handful	ܟܲܦܵܐ
deaf	ܟܲܪܵܐ
shorten	ܟܪܹܐ، ܟܪܵܝܵܐ
be angry	ܟܪܹܒ، ܟܪܵܒܵܐ
cherub	ܟܪܘܼܒܵܐ
preacher	ܟܵܪܘܿܙܵܐ
short	ܟܪܝܵܐ
ill, sick	ܟܪܝܗܵܐ
vineyard	ܟܲܪܡܵܐ
belly	ܟܲܪܣܵܐ
gluttonous	ܟܲܪܣܵܢܵܐ
energetic, striving	ܟܲܫܝܪܵܐ
reveal	ܟܫܸܦ، ܟܫܵܦܵܐ
write	ܟܬܹܒ، ܟܬܵܒܵܐ
book	ܟܬܵܒܵܐ
writer	ܟܵܬܘܿܒܵܐ
Bible	ܟܬܵܒܵܐ ܩܲܕܝܼܫܵܐ
booklet	ܟܬܵܒܘܿܢܵܐ
thorn; thistle	ܟܸܬܘܵܐ
thorny	ܟܸܬܘܵܢܵܐ
hen	ܟܬܵܝܬܵܐ

English	Chaldean	English	Chaldean
	ܠ	knead	ܠܝܫ، ܠܲܢܫܸܢ
to, for, toward	ܠ-	dough	ܠܲܝܫܵܐ
no, not	ܠܵܐ	there is not, not	ܠܲܝܒ
immortal	ܠܵܐ ܡܵܝܘܿܬܵܐ	I myself	ܠܸܠܒ
no one	ܠܵܐܐܢܵܫ	lamp	ܠܲܡܦܝܼܕܵܐ
whither	ܠܐܲܝܟܵܐ	upstairs	ܠܥܸܠ
heart	ܠܸܒܵܐ	above	ܠܥܸܠ ܡܸܢ
hearty, bold	ܠܸܒܵܢܵܐ	forever	ܠܥܵܠܲܡ
wear	ܠܒܸܫ، ܠܲܒܸܫ	chew	ܠܥܸܣ، ܠܲܥܸܣ
vestment, garment	ܠܒܘܼܫܵܐ	wave	ܠܦܵܐ
basin	ܠܲܩܢܵܐ	wavy	ܠܲܦܢܵܐ
beside	ܠܘܵܬ ܕܝܼ	no more	ܠܵܥܸܒ
ignite	ܠܗܸܐ، ܠܲܗܸܐ	vessel for oil	ܠܲܩܢܵܐ
pearl	ܠܘܼܠܐܵܐ	on top of	ܠܦܩܕ، ܠܲܩܥܸܕ
across	ܠܥܸܒܪܵܐ ܡܸܢ	loquacious	ܠܲܥܢܵܢܵܐ
tablet	ܠܘܼܚܵܐ	down	ܠܬܲܚܬ
curse	ܠܘܼܛܬܵܐ		ܡ
tongue, language	ܠܘܼܫܵܢܵܐ، ܠܸܫܵܢܵܐ	what?	ܡܵܐ
along	ܠܲܣܘܝܵܢܵܐ ܡܸܢ	what	ܡܵܐ، ܡܵܐܢܵܐ
alone	ܠܘܼܚܘܿܕ	hundred	ܡܵܐܐܵܐ
bread	ܠܲܚܡܵܐ، ܠܘܼܡܣܵܐ	food	ܡܲܐܟܘܼܠܬܵܐ
curse	ܠܝܼܛ، ܠܲܝܸܛ	speech	ܡܲܐܡܪܵܐ
night	ܠܲܝܠܹܐ	vessel	ܡܵܐܢܵܐ
lemon	ܠܲܡܘܿܢ	on behalf of	ܡܲܚܠܲܦ
coins	ܠܲܒܕܵܐ	change	ܡܲܚܠܲܦ، ܡܲܚܠܲܦܬܵܐ

brighten	ܡܒܗܪ، ܡܒܗܘܪܐ
examine	ܡܒܚܪ، ܡܒܚܘܪܐ
stop	ܡܒܛܠ، ܡܒܛܘܠܐ
because, for	ܡܒܝܕ
appear	ܡܒܝܢ، ܡܒܝܘܢܐ
confuse	ܡܒܠܒܠ، ܡܒܠܒܘܠܐ
twinkle	ܡܒܠܒܨ، ܡܒܠܒܘܨܐ
heal	ܡܒܣܡ، ܡܒܣܘܡܐ
please	ܡܒܣܡ، ܡܒܣܘܡܐ
charm	ܡܒܟܝ، ܡܒܟܘܟܝܐ
diminish	ܡܒܨܪ، ܡܒܨܘܪܐ
bubble	ܡܒܩܒܩ، ܡܒܩܒܘܩܐ
ask	ܡܒܩܪ، ܡܒܩܘܪܐ
bless	ܡܒܪܟ، ܡܒܪܘܟܐ
smile	ܡܒܪܣܡ، ܡܒܪܣܘܡܐ
polish	ܡܒܪܩ، ܡܒܪܘܩܐ
cook	ܡܒܫܠ، ܡܒܫܘܠܐ
behind	ܡܒܬܪܐ
answer	ܡܓܘܒ، ܡܓܘܘܒܐ
gather	ܡܓܡܥ، ܡܓܡܘܥܐ
rust	ܡܓܢܓܪ، ܡܓܢܓܘܪܐ
spy	ܡܓܣܣ، ܡܓܣܘܣܐ
drawer	ܡܓܪܪܐ
try, tempt	ܡܓܪܒ، ܡܓܪܘܒܐ
choose	ܡܓܒܐ، ܡܓܒܘܝܐ
magi	ܡܓܘܫܐ
thunder	ܡܓܪܓܡ، ܡܓܪܓܘܡܐ
prolong	ܡܓܪܓܥ، ܡܓܪܓܘܥܐ
govern	ܡܕܒܪ، ܡܕܒܘܪܐ
providence	ܡܕܒܪܢܘܬܐ
lie	ܡܕܓܠ، ܡܕܓܘܠܐ
button	ܡܕܓܡ، ܡܕܓܘܡܐ
praise	ܡܕܝܣ، ܡܕܝܫܐ
go insane	ܡܕܝܘܢ، ܡܕܝܘܘܢܐ
borrow	ܡܕܝܢ، ܡܕܝܘܢܐ
lend	ܡܕܝܢ، ܡܕܝܘܢܐ
clean	ܡܕܟܐ، ܡܕܟܘܝܐ
compare	ܡܕܡܐ، ܡܕܡܘܝܐ
put to sleep	ܡܕܡܟ، ܡܕܡܘܟܐ

English	Chaldean		English	Chaldean
give medicine	مَدِدْمِے، مَدِدْمَدَۥ		humility	هَمُحْدَ
school	مَدِدْهَٰ		feed	هَمُحَك، هَمُحَمَكَۥ
oppose	مَدِدْمِك، مَدِدْمَمَكَۥ		birth	هَمَكْدَ
meditation	مَدِدْعَۥ		possession	هَمَكْحَدَ
begin	مَدِعَے، مَدِعَمَۥ		teach	هَمَكك، هَمَكَمَۥ
altar	مَدِحشَۥ		blemish	هَمَهَد
citizen	مَدِبِنَۥ		cause to swear	هَمَمِد، هَمَهَمَۥ
city	مَدِبِنَۚ		promise	هَمَكِد، هَمَكَمَدِۥ
east	مَدِحشَۥ		cause to burn	هَمَمِد، هَمَسَمَدِۥ
Eastern	مَدِحشَۥ		death	هَمَمَۥ
what	مَدَۥ		plague	هَمَمَنَۥ
persecute	مَدَكِد، مَدَكِمَمَكَۥ		table	مَم
bear children	مَدَمَۥ، مَدَمَمَۥ		appetizer	مَمَۥ
believe	مَدَمِے، مَدَمَمَمَۥ		body hair	مَمَۥ
Creed	مَدَمِمَبِے		sell	مَمِے، مَمَحَمَۥ
cheer	مَدَكَمَك، مَدَكَمَمَكَۥ		increase	مَمِد، مَمَمَدِ
freezer	هَمَكِمَدِۥ		frighten	مَمِدِك، مَمَدَمَكِد
confess	هَمَدِد، هَمَدَمَۥ		join, marry	مَمَدِك، مَمَمَمَكِد
introduction	هَمَدِكَمَمَۥ		psalm	مَمَمَمَدَۥ
banana	هَمَم		hairy	مَمَنَۥ
brain	هَمَمشَۥ		plant	مَمَدَمَكَۚ
			beat	مَحِدَ، مَحشَنَۥ
			renew	مَحِدِے، مَحِدِمَمَمَۥ

123

English	Chaldean
show	ܡܚܘܐ، ܡܚܘܝܐ
show	ܡܚܘܐ، ܡܚܘܝܐ
united	ܡܚܘܕܐ
weak	ܡܚܝܠܐ
talk	ܡܚܟܐ، ܡܚܟܝܐ
wash	ܡܚܠܠ، ܡܚܠܘܠܐ
save, deliver	ܡܚܠܨ، ܡܚܠܘܨܐ
savior	ܡܚܠܨܢܐ
preserve	ܡܚܡܐ، ܡܚܡܝܐ
forgive	ܡܚܣܐ، ܡܚܣܝܐ
graduate	ܡܚܪܓ، ܡܚܪܘܓܐ
reckon	ܡܚܫܒ، ܡܚܫܘܒܐ
wave	ܡܚܫܘܠܐ
arrive	ܡܛܐ، ܡܛܝܢܐ
kitchen	ܡܛܒܚ
printing press	ܡܛܒܥܬܐ
circumcise	ܡܛܗܪ، ܡܛܗܘܪܐ
roast	ܡܛܘܐ، ܡܛܘܝܐ
arrange	ܡܛܟܣ، ܡܛܟܘܣܐ
destroy	ܡܛܠܩ، ܡܛܠܘܩܐ
spoon	ܡܛܥܡܢܝܬܐ
bury	ܡܛܡܪ، ܡܛܡܘܪܐ
play	ܡܛܝܠ، ܡܛܝܘܠܐ
restaurant	ܡܛܥܡ
stick	ܡܛܦܐ، ܡܛܦܘܝܐ
flicker	ܡܛܦܛܦ، ܡܛܦܛܘܦܐ
airport	ܡܛܪܐ
rain	ܡܝܛܪܐ
applaud	ܡܛܪܦ، ܡܛܪܘܦܐ
conceal	ܡܛܫܐ، ܡܛܫܝܐ
water	ܡܝܐ
imprisoned	ܡܝܘܣܪܐ
mortal	ܡܝܘܬܐ
dinner table	ܡܝܙ ܕܐܟܠܐ
mile	ܡܝܠܐ
monkey	ܡܝܡܘܢ
vessel	ܡܐܢܐ
watery	ܡܝܢܐ
honor	ܡܝܩܪ، ܡܝܩܘܪܐ
die	ܡܝܬ، ܡܝܬܐ
toss	ܡܟܦܟܦ، ܡܟܦܟܘܦܐ

call ܡܟܪܐ، ܡܟܪܘܝܐ
meek, gentle ܡܟܝܟܐ
stop ܡܟܠܐ، ܡܟܠܘܝܐ
crown ܡܟܠܠ، ܟܠܘܠܐ
perfect ܡܟܡܠ، ܡܟܡܘܠܐ
sweep, gather ܡܟܢܫ، ܡܟܢܘܫܐ
tax-gatherer ܡܟܣܐ
cover ܡܟܣܐ، ܡܟܣܘܝܐ
be lazy ܡܟܣܠ، ܡܟܣܘܠܐ
sink ܡܟܣܟܐ
become dirty ܡܟܦܠ، ܡܟܦܘܠܐ
purificator (mass) ܡܟܦܪܢܐ
preach ܡܟܪܙ، ܡܟܪܘܙܐ
library ܡܟܬܒܬܐ
fill ܡܠܐ، ܡܠܝܐ
angel ܡܠܐܟܐ
encourage ܡܠܒܒ، ܡܠܒܘܒܐ
clothe ܡܠܒܫ، ܡܠܒܘܫܐ
salt ܡܠܚܐ
full ܡܠܝܐ، ܡܠܝܬܐ
rational ܡܠܝܠܐ
king ܡܠܟܐ
kingdom ܡܠܟܘܬܐ
queen ܡܠܟܬܐ
chew ܡܠܥܣ، ܡܠܥܘܣܐ
stadium ܡܠܥܒ
pollute ܡܠܟܠܟ، ܡܠܟܠܘܟܐ
teacher ܡܠܦܢܐ
doctrine, teaching ܡܠܦܢܘܬܐ
mother ܡܡܐ
speech ܡܡܠܠܐ
tell a story ܡܡܬܠ، ܡܡܬܘܠܐ
play ܡܡܬܠܬܐ
from ܡܢ
who ܡܢ، ܡܢܝ
count ܡܢܐ، ܡܢܝܢܐ
thing ܡܢܕܝ
from the beginning ܡܢܕܪܫ
clean ܡܢܕܦ، ܡܢܕܘܦܐ
comment ܡܢܗܪ، ܡܢܗܘܪܐ
plead ܡܢܘܝܐ، ܡܢܘܢܘܝܐ
be sick ܡܢܘܟܠܐ
raise from the dead ܡܢܚܡ، ܡܢܚܘܡܐ
number ܡܢܝܢܐ

bowl	ܡܝܼܟ݂ܲܦ݂ܵܐ
manna	ܡܲܢܵܐ
cuss at	ܡܲܢܝܸܠ، ܡܲܢܘܼܠܹܐ
hesitate	ܡܲܢܣܸܣ، ܡܲܢܣܘܼܣܹܐ
make forget	ܡܲܢܫܹܐ، ܡܲܢܫܘܼܝܹܐ
kiss	ܡܢܲܫܘܼܩܝܼܬ݂ܵܐ
wash clothes	ܡܣܲܚܹܐ، ܡܣܵܚܵܐ
satisfy	ܡܣܲܒܸܥ، ܡܣܲܒܘܼܥܹܐ
endure	ܡܣܲܝܒܸܪ، ܡܣܲܝܒܘܼܪܹܐ
needy, poor	ܡܣܟܝܼܢܵܐ
lose	ܡܣܲܟܸܪ، ܡܣܲܟܘܼܪܹܐ
despise	ܡܣܲܠܹܐ، ܡܣܲܠܘܼܝܹܐ
deliver	ܡܣܲܦܹܐ، ܡܣܲܦܘܼܝܹܐ
empty	ܡܣܲܦܸܩ، ܡܣܲܦܘܼܩܹܐ
traveling	ܡܣܲܦܸܪ، ܡܣܲܦܘܼܪܹܐ
traveler	ܡܣܲܦܪܵܢܵܐ
adorn	ܡܣܲܩܸܠ، ܡܣܲܩܘܼܠܹܐ
comb, brush	ܡܣܪܵܩܵܐ
toothbrush	ܡܣܪܵܩܵܐ ܕܟܵܟܹ̈ܐ
let enter	ܡܲܥܒܸܪ، ܡܲܥܒܘܼܪܹܐ
annoy	ܡܲܥܩܹܐ، ܡܲܥܩܘܼܝܹܐ
lament	ܡܥܲܕܸܕ، ܡܥܲܕܘܼܕܹܐ
straighten	ܡܥܲܕܸܠ، ܡܥܲܕܘܼܠܹܐ
late	ܡܥܘܼܟ݂ܵܒ݂ܵܐ
yell	ܡܥܲܝܸܛ، ܡܥܲܝܘܼܛܹܐ
raise	ܡܲܥܠܹܐ، ܡܲܥܠܘܼܝܹܐ
entrance	ܡܲܥܠܬ݂ܵܐ
baptize	ܡܲܥܡܸܕ، ܡܲܥܡܘܼܕܹܐ
baptism	ܡܲܥܡܘܼܕܝܼܬ݂ܵܐ
dwelling place	ܡܲܥܡܪܵܐ
delay	ܡܥܲܟܸܒ، ܡܥܲܟܘܼܒܹܐ
West	ܡܲܥܪܒܵܐ
western	ܡܲܥܪܒܵܝܵܐ
chase	ܡܲܥܪܸܩ، ܡܲܥܪܘܼܩܹܐ
make old	ܡܲܥܬܸܩ، ܡܲܥܬܘܼܩܹܐ
divide	ܡܦܲܠܸܓ، ܡܦܲܠܘܼܓܹܐ
put out, expel	ܡܦܲܠܸܛ، ܡܦܲܠܘܼܛܹܐ
please, gladden	ܡܦܲܨܸܚ، ܡܦܲܨܘܼܚܹܐ
regret	ܡܦܲܫܸܡ، ܡܦܲܫܘܼܡܹܐ
translate	ܡܦܲܫܸܩ، ܡܦܲܫܘܼܩܹܐ
interpreter	ܡܦܲܫܩܵܢܵܐ
watch	ܡܨܲܕܹܐ، ܡܨܲܕܘܼܝܹܐ

pray	ܡܨܲܠܸܐ، ܡܨܲܠܘܼܝܹܐ
flow, pour out	ܡܨܲܝܸܠ، ܡܨܲܝܘܼܠܹܐ
mediator	ܡܨܲܥܝܵܢܵܐ
listen	ܡܨܲܝܸܬ، ܡܨܲܝܘܼܬܹܐ
everything that	ܡܲܩܵܐ ܕ
how much	ܡܲܩܵܐ
so long as	ܡܲܩܲܕ
anticipate, precede	ܡܩܲܕܸܡ، ܡܩܲܕܘܼܡܹܐ
introduction	ܡܩܲܕܡܲܝܬܵܐ
measure, respect	ܡܩܲܕܸܪ، ܡܩܲܕܘܼܪܹܐ
sanctify, consecrate	ܡܩܲܕܸܫ، ܡܩܲܕܘܼܫܹܐ
cut up	ܡܩܲܛܸܥ، ܡܩܲܛܘܼܥܹܐ
peel	ܡܩܲܠܸܦ، ܡܩܲܠܘܼܦܹܐ
lighten, expedite	ܡܩܲܠܸܠ، ܡܩܲܠܘܼܠܹܐ
raise	ܡܲܩܝܸܡ، ܡܲܩܡܘܼܝܹܐ
convince	ܡܲܩܢܸܥ، ܡܲܩܢܘܼܥܹܐ
scissors	ܡܲܩܨܵܐ
intention	ܡܲܩܨܵܕ
cut up	ܡܩܲܨܩܸܨ، ܡܩܲܨܩܘܼܨܹܐ
strive, fight	ܡܩܲܬܸܠ، ܡܩܲܬܘܼܠܹܐ

zealous	ܡܵܪܵܐ ܛܢܵܢܘܼܬܵܐ
valuable	ܡܵܪܵܐ ܛܝܼܡܵܐ
lord; master	ܡܵܪܵܐ
mirror	ܡܪܵܝܵܐ
educate, grow	ܡܪܲܒܸܐ، ܡܪܲܒܘܼܝܹܐ
box, womb	ܡܪܲܒܥܵܐ
beseech	ܡܪܲܓܸܐ، ܡܪܲܓܘܼܝܹܐ
pasture	ܡܲܪܓܵܐ
instruction	ܡܪܲܕܘܼܬܵܐ
rebellious	ܡܵܪܘܿܕܵܐ
humiliate	ܡܪܲܘܸܠ، ܡܪܲܘܘܼܠܹܐ
bold	ܡܪܲܚܵܐ
have mercy	ܡܪܲܚܸܡ، ܡܪܲܚܘܼܡܹܐ
compassion	ܡܪܲܚܡܢܘܼܬܵܐ
my Lord	ܡܵܪܝ
Lord God	ܡܵܪܝܵܐ
injured	ܡܪܝܼܥܵܐ
bitter	ܡܪܝܼܪܵܐ
compound	ܡܪܲܟܒܵܐ
our Lord	ܡܵܪܲܢ
of our Lord	ܡܵܪܲܢܵܝܵܐ
be hurt	ܡܪܸܥ، ܡܪܵܥܵܐ
injury	ܡܪܥܵܐ
stomachache	ܡܲܪܥܵܐ ܕܟܲܪܣܵܐ
headache	ܡܲܪܥܵܐ ܕܪܹܫܵܐ

English	Chaldean	English	Chaldean
flock, diocese	ܡܲܪܥܝܼܬ݂ܐ	pour out	ܡܲܫܦܹܥ، ܡܲܫܦܘܼܥܹܐ
stew	ܡܲܪܩܐ	plead	ܡܲܬ݂ܩܲܠܸܩ،
boil water	ܡܲܪܬ݂ܲܚ، ܡܲܪܬ݂ܘܼܚܹܐ		ܡܲܬ݂ܩܲܠܸܩ ܒܹܐ
wipe	ܡܫܹܐ، ܡܲܫܝܹܐ	begin	ܡܲܫܪܹܐ، ܡܲܫܪܘܼܝܹܐ
glorify	ܡܲܫܒܲܚ،	water, give drink	ܡܲܫܩܹܐ، ܡܲܫܩܘܼܝܹܐ
	ܡܲܫܒܘܼܚܹܐ	feast	ܡܸܫܬܘܼܬ݂ܐ
send	ܡܲܫܕܸܪ، ܡܲܫܕܘܼܪܹܐ	village	ܡܵܬ݂ܐ
desire	ܡܲܣܚܸܦ، ܡܲܣܚܘܼܦܹܐ	bring	ܡܵܬܹܐ، ܡܲܡܬܘܼܝܹܐ
anoint	ܡܫܲܚ، ܡܲܫܚܹܐ	Incarnation	ܡܸܬ݂ܒܲܪܢܫܵܢܘܼܬ݂ܐ
oil	ܡܸܫܚܐ	prove	ܡܲܚܬ݂ܹܐ، ܡܲܚܬ݂ܘܼܝܹܐ
alter	ܡܲܫܚܸܠܸܦ،	everlasting	ܡܬܘܼܡܵܝܐ
	ܡܲܫܚܸܠܘܼܦܹܐ	consider	ܡܲܚܫܸܒ݂،
oily	ܡܸܫܚܵܢܐ		ܡܲܚܫܘܼܒ݂ܹܐ
eraser	ܡܲܚܝܵܢܐ	delay	ܡܲܚܣܸܪ، ܡܲܚܣܘܼܪܹܐ
Christ	ܡܫܝܼܚܐ	proverb	ܡܲܬ݂ܠܐ
Christian	ܡܫܝܼܚܵܝܐ	convert	ܡܲܬ݂ܠܡܸܕ،
become dirty	ܡܲܬ݂ܚܹܐ،		ܡܲܬ݂ܠܡܘܼܕܹܐ
	ܡܲܬ݂ܚܘܼܝܹܐ	hang, suspend	ܡܲܬ݂ܠܹܐ، ܡܲܬ݂ܠܘܼܝܹܐ
busy oneself	ܡܫܲܥܒܸܕ، ܡܫܲܥܒܘܼܕܹܐ	complete	ܡܲܫܡܸܙ، ܡܲܫܡܘܼܙܹܐ
serve in liturgy	ܡܫܲܡܸܫ، ܡܫܲܡܘܼܫܹܐ	trespass	ܡܲܫܠܸܕ، ܡܲܫܠܘܼܕܹܐ
move away	ܡܲܫܢܹܐ، ܡܲܫܢܘܼܝܹܐ	whisper	ܡܲܪܥܸܙ، ܡܲܪܥܘܼܙܹܐ
dangle	ܡܲܫܬܸܠܐ، ܡܲܫܬܸܠܬ݂ܹܐ		
suffer	ܡܲܫܬܲܠܸܕ، ܡܲܫܬܲܠܕܘܼܕܹܐ		

ܢ

fountain	ܢܒܘܥܐ
prophet	ܢܒܝܐ
vow	ܢܕܪܐ
become clean	ܢܕܟ، ܢܕܟܐ
river	ܢܗܪܐ، ܢܗܪܐ
grandson	ܢܘܓܐ
granddaughter	ܢܘܓܬܐ
commentary	ܢܘܗܪܐ
light	ܢܘܗܪܐ
resurrection	ܢܘܚܡܐ
stranger	ܢܘܟܪܝܐ
sleep	ܢܘܡܐ
fish	ܢܘܢܐ، ܢܘܢܬܐ
hole	ܢܘܩܒܐ
dot	ܢܘܩܙܐ
fire	ܢܘܪܐ
stream	ܢܚܠܐ
descend	ܢܚܬ، ܢܚܬܐ
drop	ܢܛܘܦܬܐ
guard	ܢܛܪ، ܢܛܪܐ
pipe	ܢܝ
rest	ܢܝܚ، ܢܝܚܐ
slowly	ܢܝܚܐܝܬ
Nineveh	ܢܝܢܘܐ
April	ܢܝܣܢ
shy, modest	ܢܟܦܐ
shy	ܢܟܦ، ܢܟܦܐ
tiger	ܢܡܪܐ
grandmother	ܢܢܐ
temptation	ܢܣܝܘܢܐ
grace	ܢܥܡܐ
fall	ܢܦܠ، ܢܦܠܐ
go out	ܢܦܩ، ܢܦܩܐ
soul	ܢܦܫܐ
noble	ܢܨܝܚܐ
female	ܢܩܒܐ
feminine	ܢܩܒܝܐ
thin	ܢܩܕ، ܢܩܕܐ
thin	ܢܩܝܕܐ
person	ܢܫܐ
forget	ܢܫܐ، ܢܫܝܐ
kiss	ܢܫܘܩܬܐ
eagle	ܢܫܪܐ
ear	ܢܬܐ

ܣ

silver	ܣܐܡܐ
grandfather, old man	ܣܒܐ
grow old	ܣܐܒ، ܣܒܝܐ
be satisfied	ܣܒܥ، ܣܒܥܐ

English	Chaldean	English	Chaldean
hope	ܣܲܒ݂ܪܵܐ	movie	ܣܸܢܸܡܵܐ
gospel	ܣܒ݂ܵܪܬܵܐ	sword	ܣܲܝܦܵܐ
grandmother, old woman	ܣܵܒ݂ܬܵܐ	calendar	ܣܸܩܘܿܡܵܐ
adore, worship	ܣܓ݂ܝܼܕ، ܣܵܓ݂ܹܕ	car	ܣܹܩܪܵܐ
witness	ܣܵܗܕܵܐ	ambulance	ܣܹܩܪܵܐ ܕܚܛܵܝܹ̈ܐ
testify, be martyred	ܣܗܝܼܕ، ܣܵܗܹܕ	knife	ܣܲܟܝܼܢܵܐ
moon	ܣܲܗܪܵܐ	ignorant	ܣܲܟ݂ܠܵܐ
crescent	ܣܲܗܪܘܿܢܵܐ	drain board	ܣܲܟ݂ܵܐ ܕܡܵܐܢܹ̈ܐ
finger	ܣܘܿܒ݂ܥܵܐ	poison	ܣܲܡܵܐ
Annunciation, Advent	ܣܘܿܒ݂ܵܪܵܐ	lose sight	ܣܡܝܼ، ܣܵܡܹܐ
vernacular	ܣܘܿܪܬ݂ܵܐ	red	ܣܘܿܡܵܩܵܐ
Ascension	ܣܘܿܠܵܩܵܐ	poisonous	ܣܲܡܵܢܵܐ
ruby	ܣܘܿܡܵܩܬܵܐ	hate	ܣܢܹܐ، ܣܵܢܹܐ
need	ܣܘܿܢܩܵܢܵܐ	box	ܣܲܢܕܘܿܩܵܐ
horse	ܣܘܿܣܵܐ	hateful	ܣܢܵܝܵܐ
knight	ܣܘܿܣܵܢܵܐ	require	ܣܢܝܼܩ، ܣܵܢܹܩ
mare	ܣܘܿܣܬܵܐ	sacristan	ܣܲܥܘܿܪܵܐ
calendar	ܣܘܿܪܓ݂ܵܕ݂ܵܐ	pillow	ܣܲܥܕܝܼܢܵܐ
swim, bathe	ܣܚܹܐ، ܣܵܚܹܐ	mouthful	ܣܲܦܣܵܪܵܐ
swimmer	ܣܵܚܵܝܵܐ	tatter	ܣܩܝܼܩ، ܣܵܩܹܩ
go (imperative)	ܣܲܩ	empty	ܣܪܝܼܩ، ܣܵܪܹܩ
old age	ܣܲܝܒ݂ܘܿܬ݂ܵܐ	wait	ܣܟ݂ܹܐ، ܣܵܟ݂ܹܐ
treasure	ܣܝܼܡܬ݂ܵܐ	book	ܣܸܦܪܵܐ
filth	ܣܝܼܵܢܵܐ	scribe	ܣܵܦܪܵܐ
		lip	ܣܸܦܬ݂ܵܐ

adornment	ܣܶܡܠܳܐ
rot	ܣܪܶܐ، ܣܪܳܝܳܐ
seraph	ܣܪܳܦܳܐ
pillow	ܣܳܡܟܬܳܐ
winter	ܣܶܬܘܳܐ
covering	ܣܶܬܪܳܐ
	ܥ
feast day	ܥܺܐܕܳܐ
servant, slave	ܥܰܒܕܳܐ
do, make	ܥܒܶܕ، ܥܒܳܕܳܐ
transitory	ܥܳܒܽܘܪܳܐ
pass	ܥܒܰܪ، ܥܒܳܪܳܐ
entrance, crossing	ܥܶܒܪܬܳܐ
will	ܥܶܓܘܢܳܐ
wonder, miracle	ܥܓܘܒܬܳܐ
accustomed	ܥܝܺܕܳܐ
time	ܥܶܕܳܢܳܐ
church	ܥܺܕܬܳܐ
ecclesiastical	ܥܺܕܬܳܢܳܐ
suffering	ܥܘܼܕܳܒܳܐ
aid	ܥܘܼܕܪܳܢܳܐ
commemoration	ܥܘܼܗܕܳܢܳܐ
evil	ܥܰܘܠܳܐ
deep	ܥܘܼܡܩܳܐ
dwelling	ܥܘܼܡܪܳܐ
help	ܥܘܼܕܪ
ewe	ܥܘܼܢܳܐ
responsary	ܥܘܼܢܺܝܬܳܐ
dirt	ܥܘܼܦܪܳܐ
earthy	ܥܘܼܦܪܳܢܳܐ
goat	ܥܶܙܳܐ
beloved	ܥܙܺܝܙܳܐ
thigh	ܥܶܛܡܳܐ
cloud of incense	ܥܶܛܪܳܐ
cloud	ܥܢܳܢܳܐ
cloudy	ܥܢܳܢܳܢܳܐ
ring	ܥܶܙܩܬܳܐ
eye	ܥܰܝܢܳܐ
constrain, be constrained, in pain	ܥܺܝܩ، ܥܳܩܳܐ
angel, watcher	ܥܺܝܪܳܐ
on, over	ܥܰܠ
ascend	ܥܠܶܐ، ܥܳܠܠܳܐ
upon	ܥܠܰܝ
high	ܥܠܘܼܝܳܐ
lane	ܥܶܠܘܟܳܐ
high	ܥܶܠܳܝܳܐ
eternal	ܥܳܠܰܡ
world	ܥܳܠܡܳܐ
secular	ܥܳܠܡܳܢܳܐ

eternal	ܥܠܡܝܢ
cause	ܥܠܬܐ
with	ܥܡ، ܥܡܕ
nation, people	ܥܡܡܐ
paternal uncle	ܥܡܐ
be baptized	ܥܡܕ، ܥܡܕܐ
deep	ܥܡܘܩܐ
workman	ܥܡܠܐ
dwell	ܥܡܪ، ܥܡܪܐ
fleece, wool	ܥܡܪܐ
paternal aunt	ܥܡܬܐ
grape	ܥܢܒܐ
dead	ܥܢܝܕܐ
could	ܥܢܢܐ
soldier	ܥܣܟܪܐ
difficult	ܥܣܩܐ
left	ܥܣܪܐ
ten	ܥܣܪܐ
twenty	ܥܣܪܝܢ
hard	ܥܨܢܐ
afternoon	ܥܨܪܘܬܐ
mouse	ܥܩܘܒܪܐ
barren	ܥܩܪܐ
root	ܥܩܪܐ
hold	ܥܕܪ، ܥܕܪܐ
Friday	ܥܪܘܒܬܐ
fugitive	ܥܪܘܩܐ
run	ܥܪܩ، ܥܪܩܐ
dinner	ܥܫܝܐ
old	ܥܬܝܩܐ
rich	ܥܬܝܪܐ
	ܦ
so-and-so	ܦܠܢܐ
pepper	ܦܠܦܠܐ
fruit	ܦܐܪܐ
face	ܦܐܬܐ
rude	ܦܐܬܢܐ
body	ܦܓܪܐ
bodily	ܦܓܪܢܐ
bodily	ܦܓܪܢܝܐ
phlegm	ܦܘܕܐ
countencance	ܦܘܪܐ
serious	ܦܘܪܢܐ
wind, breath	ܦܘܚܐ
work, labor	ܦܘܠܚܢܐ
mouth	ܦܘܡܐ
answer	ܦܘܢܝܐ
nose	ܦܘܩܐ
command	ܦܘܩܕܢܐ
salvation	ܦܘܪܩܢܐ

reasoning	ܦܘܼܪܵܫܵܐ
orange	ܦܘܼܪܬܩܵܠ
orange (color)	ܦܘܼܪܬܩܵܠܵܝܵܐ
translation	ܦܘܼܫܵܩܵܐ
cool	ܦܝܼܫܵܪܵܐ
cool, be appeased	ܦܝܼܫ، ܦܝܵܫܵܐ
elephant	ܦܝܼܠܵܐ
paten	ܦܝܼܢܟܵܐ
philosopher	ܦܝܼܠܵܣܘܿܦܵܐ
dirty	ܦܝܫ
remain	ܦܝܼܫ، ܦܝܵܫܵܐ
bland	ܦܲܟ݂ܵܐ
divide	ܦܠܸܓ݂، ܦܠܵܓ݂ܵܐ
half	ܦܠܸܓ݂ܵܐ
noon	ܦܠܸܓ݂ܵܐ ܕܝܘܿܡܵܐ
downtown	ܦܠܸܓ݂ܵܐ ܕܡܵܬܵܐ
mid-Lent	ܦܠܸܓ݂ܵܗ
division	ܦܘܼܠܵܓ݂ܵܐ
middle	ܦܲܠܓܵܝܵܐ
deceitful	ܦܲܠܘܿܬܵܐ
work	ܦܠܝܼܚ، ܦܠܵܚܵܐ
worker	ܦܵܠܚܵܐ
go out	ܦܠܝܼܛ، ܦܠܵܛܵܐ
crooked	ܦܠܝܼܩܵܐ
twist	ܦܠܝܼܬ، ܦܠܵܬܵܐ

Pentecost	ܦܸܢܛܹܩܘܿܣܛܹܐ
pants	ܦܢܛܪܘܿܢ
chapter	ܦܲܣܘܿܩܵܐ
worker	ܦܥܵܠܵܐ
lamb	ܦܲܥܪܵܐ
Pope	ܦܲܦܵܐ
rejoice	ܦܨܝܼܚ، ܦܨܵܚܵܐ
Passover	ܦܸܨܚܵܐ
joy	ܦܨܝܼܚܘܼܬܵܐ
happy	ܦܨܝܼܚܵܐ
meat	ܦܸܣܪܵܐ
frog	ܦܲܩܵܐ
command	ܦܩܝܼܕ، ܦܩܵܕܵܐ
tadpole	ܦܩܝܼܒܬܵܐ
explode	ܦܩܝܼܥ، ܦܩܵܥܵܐ
crack	ܦܩܵܥܵܐ
neck	ܦܩܵܪܬܵܐ
feather	ܦܲܪܵܐ
money	ܦܵܪܹܐ
curtain	ܦܲܪܕܵܐ
flying	ܦܪܘܼܚܵܐ
steel	ܦܪܘܼܠܵܕ
piece	ܦܸܪܓܵܐ
pay, pay back	ܦܪܝܼܥ، ܦܪܵܥܵܐ
reward	ܦܘܼܪܥܵܢܵܐ

save	ܦܪܩ، ܦܪܩܐ
separate	ܦܪܫ، ܦܪܫܐ
distinction	ܦܪܫܘܢܐ
lukewarm	ܦܫܘܪܐ
extend, spread out	ܦܫܛ، ܦܫܛܐ
stretch out	ܦܫܛ، ܦܫܛܐ
simple	ܦܫܝܛܐ
branch	ܦܫܟܐ
melt	ܦܫܪ، ܦܫܪܐ
face	ܦܬܐ
paten, table	ܦܬܘܪܐ
open	ܦܬܚ، ܦܬܚܐ
wide	ܦܬܝܐ
open	ܦܬܝܚܐ
turn	ܦܬܠ، ܦܬܠܐ
understand	ܦܗܡ، ܦܗܡܐ
chance, opportunity	ܦܘܪܨܐ
pass	ܦܝܬ، ܦܬܬܐ
dress	ܦܣܛܢܐ
poor	ܦܩܝܪܐ
abundant	ܦܪܝܫܐ
brush	ܦܪܟܐ
stove	ܦܪܢ

ܨ

chalkboard	ܨܒܘܪܐ
dye	ܨܒܥ، ܨܒܥܐ
contentment	ܨܒܪܐ
thirst	ܨܗܐ، ܨܗܝܐ
thirst	ܨܗܘܐ
preparation	ܨܘܒܬܐ
house shoes	ܨܘܠܐ
fast, Lent	ܨܘܡܐ
section	ܨܚܚܐ
plate	ܨܚܢܐ
hunt	ܨܝܕ، ܨܝܕܐ
fisherman, huntsman	ܨܝܕܐ
hunting	ܨܝܕܐ
fast	ܨܝܡ، ܨܝܡܐ
crucify	ܨܠܒ، ܨܠܒܐ
prayer	ܨܠܘܬܐ
cross	ܨܠܝܒܐ
image	ܨܠܡܐ
splendor	ܨܡܚܐ
tray	ܨܝܢܝܐ
banquet	ܨܦܪܐ
clean, pure	ܨܦܝܐ
purity	ܨܦܝܘܬܐ
sparrow	ܨܦܪܐ
tomorrow	ܨܦܪܐ
cockroach, grasshopper	ܨܨܪܐ

tear ܬܪܸܐ، ܬܪܵܝܵܐ

misbehave ܬܪܸܣ، ܬܪܵܣܵܐ

absorb ܬܪܸܦ، ܬܪܵܦܵܐ

ܩ

burial ܩܒܘܼܪܬܵܐ

robe ܩܲܒܵܐ

receive, accept ܩܒܸܠ، ܩܒܵܠܵܐ

bury ܩܒܸܪ، ܩܒܵܪܵܐ

tomb ܩܲܒܪܵܐ

holy of holies, sanctuary ܩܕܘܼܫ ܩܘܼܕܫܹ̈ܐ

holy, saint ܩܲܕܝܼܫܵܐ

before, in front of ܩܲܕܵܡ

precede ܩܲܕܸܡ، ܩܲܕܘܼܡܹܐ

front ܩܲܕܡܵܐ

first ܩܲܕܡܵܝܵܐ

morning ܩܲܕܡܵܬ݂ܵܐ

key ܩܠܝܼܕܵܐ

before, in front of ܩܕܵܡܝܼ

coffee ܩܲܗܘܵܐ

coffee colored ܩܲܗܘܵܝܵܐ

classroom ܩܘܼܒܝܼ ܕܝܼܕܥܬܵܐ

reception, acceptance ܩܘܼܒܵܠܵܐ

Hallowing of the Church ܩܘܼܕܵܫ ܥܹܕܬܵܐ

hallowing ܩܘܼܕܵܫܵܐ

holy ܩܘܼܕܫܵܐ

jump ܩܘܼܛ، ܩܘܼܛܵܐ

ash ܩܘܼܛܡܵܐ

gray ܩܘܼܛܡܵܢܵܐ

establishment ܩܘܼܝܵܡܵܐ

height ܩܘܼܡܬ݂ܵܐ

shoes ܩܘܼܢܕܵܪܹ̈ܐ

jar ܩܘܼܩܬ݂ܵܐ

offering, Eucharist ܩܘܼܪܒܵܢܵܐ

teapot ܩܘܼܪܝ

root ܩܘܼܪܡܵܐ

cat ܩܲܛܘܼ

murderer ܩܵܛܘܿܠܵܐ

kill ܩܛܸܠ، ܩܛܵܠܵܐ

murderer ܩܲܛܠܵܐ

ashes ܩܛܡܵܐ

gray ܩܛܡܵܢܵܐ

cut ܩܛܸܥ، ܩܛܵܥܵܐ

fraction ܩܛܵܥܵܐ

pick ܩܛܸܦ، ܩܛܵܦܵܐ

tie, wreathe ܩܛܸܪ، ܩܛܵܪܵܐ

arch ܩܸܛܪܵܐ

knot ܩܸܛܪܵܐ

officer ܩܲܝܘܼܡܵܐ

summer ܩܲܝܛܵܐ

rise	ܩܐܡ، ܩܝܡܐ
resurrection	ܩܝܡܬܐ
wood	ܩܝܣܐ
cool	ܩܐܪ، ܩܝܪܐ
harp	ܩܝܬܪܐ
voice	ܩܠܐ
fry	ܩܠܐ، ܩܠܝܐ
turn over	ܩܠܒ، ܩܠܒܐ
quick, small	ܩܠܝܠܐ
little	ܩܠܝܠ
cell	ܩܠܝܬܐ
pen	ܩܠܡܐ
be peeled	ܩܠܦ، ܩܠܦܐ
skin, rind, crust	ܩܠܦܐ
move	ܩܠܩ، ܩܠܩܐ
flour	ܩܡܚܐ
locust	ܩܡܨܐ
acquire	ܩܢܐ
nest	ܩܢܐ
lamp	ܩܢܕܝܠܐ
individuality	ܩܢܘܡܐ
proper	ܩܢܘܡܝܐ
canon, rule	ܩܢܘܢܐ
canonical	ܩܢܘܢܝܐ
center	ܩܢܛܪܘܢ
centurion	ܩܢܛܪܘܢܐ
sanctuary	ܩܢܟܐ
be convinced	ܩܢܥ، ܩܢܥܐ
coat	ܩܦܘܛ
hug	ܩܦܠ، ܩܦܠܐ
locked	ܩܦܝܠܐ
little	ܩܨܪܐ
fracture	ܩܨܪ، ܩܨܪܐ
palace	ܩܨܪܐ
story	ܩܨܬܐ
head, skull	ܩܪܐ
call, read	ܩܪܐ، ܩܪܝܐ
approach	ܩܪܒ، ܩܪܒܐ
turtle	ܩܪܓܠܐ
reader	ܩܪܘܝܐ
bite, gnaw	ܩܪܛ، ܩܪܛܐ
bite	ܩܪܛܐ
by, near	ܩܪܝܒܐ
godfather	ܩܪܝܒܐ
near	ܩܪܝܒܐ ܡܢ
godmother	ܩܪܝܒܬܐ
reading	ܩܪܝܢܐ
cold	ܩܪܝܪܐ
wrap	ܩܪܡ، ܩܪܡܐ
horn	ܩܪܢܐ

squash	ܩܲܪܥܵܐ
skull	ܩܲܪܩܲܦܬܵܐ
cold	ܩܲܪܬܵܐ
priest, elder	ܩܲܫܵܐ
seminarian	ܩܲܫܘܼܢܵܐ
become fat	ܩܫܹܗ، ܩܫܵܗܵܐ
bow	ܩܹܫܬܵܐ
stick, handle	ܩܲܬܵܐ
Catholicos-Patriarch	ܩܲܬܘܿܠܝܼܩܵܐ
catholic	ܩܲܬܘܿܠܝܼܩܝܼ
	ܪ
arrangement	ܪܸܨܦܵܐ
archangel	ܪܲܒ ܡܲܠܲܐܟ̈ܐ
large, great	ܪܲܒܵܐ
grow	ܪܒܹܐ، ܪܒܵܝܵܐ
ten thousand; a myriad	ܪܸܒܘܿ، ܪܸܒܘܼܬܵܐ
teacher	ܪܲܒܝܼ
spring	ܪܒܝܼܥܵܐ
fourth, a quarter	ܪܒܝܼܥܵܝܵܐ
monk	ܪܲܒܵܢ
nun	ܪܲܒܵܢܬܵܐ، ܪܲܒܵܢܝܼܬܵܐ
feel	ܪܓܹܫ، ܪܓܵܫܵܐ
feeling	ܪܸܓܫܵܐ
persecution	ܪܕܘܼܦܝܵܐ
pledge	ܪܸܗܒܘܿܢܵܐ
get drunk	ܪܘܹܐ، ܪܘܵܝܵܐ
noise	ܪܘܼܒܵܐ
anger	ܪܘܼܓܙܵܐ
earthquake	ܪܘܼܕܵܢܵܐ
rejoice	ܪܘܹܙ، ܪܘܵܙܵܐ
widen, spread out	ܪܘܹܚ، ܪܘܵܚܵܐ
spirit	ܪܘܼܚܵܐ
spiritual	ܪܘܼܚܵܢܵܝܵܐ
drunkard	ܪܵܘܝܵܐ
expansion	ܪܘܼܝܚܘܼܬܵܐ
structure	ܪܘܼܟܵܒܵܐ
aspiration, softening	ܪܘܼܟܵܟܵܐ
height	ܪܘܼܡܵܐ
spear	ܪܘܼܡܚܵܐ
hill	ܪܵܡܬܵܐ
shoulder	ܪܘܼܦܬܵܐ
spittle	ܪܘܼܩܵܐ
sign	ܪܘܼܫܡܵܐ
rice	ܪܸܙܵܐ
far	ܪܚܘܼܩܵܐ
mercy	ܪܚܡܹܐ
avoid, go far away	ܪܚܹܩ، ܪܚܵܩܵܐ
walk, creep	ܪܚܹܫ، ܪܚܵܫܵܐ
fragrance	ܪܹܝܚܵܐ
sweet-smelling	ܪܝܼܚܵܢܵܐ

spit	ܪܩ، ܪܩܩܐ
syliva	ܪܩܐ
ride	ܪܟܒ، ܪܟܒܐ
rider	ܪܟܒܐ
soft, tender	ܪܟܝܟܐ
soften	ܪܟܟ، ܪܟܟܐ
high, exalted	ܪܡܐ
arrogance	ܪܡܘܬܐ
sign	ܪܡܙ، ܪܡܙܐ
indication, sign	ܪܡܙܐ
symbolic	ܪܡܙܢܝܐ
proud	ܪܡܢܐ
evening prayer	ܪܡܫܐ
good	ܪܕܝܐ، ܪܕܝܐ
shepherd	ܪܥܝܐ
shake, shiver	ܪܥܠ، ܪܥܠܠܐ
thunder	ܪܥܡܐ
shelf	ܪܦܐ
loosen	ܪܦܐ، ܪܦܝܐ
moment	ܪܦܦܐ
dance	ܪܩܕ، ܪܩܕܐ
dancer	ܪܩܕܐ
firmament, sky	ܪܩܝܥܐ
fine, thin	ܪܩܝܩܐ
on, upon	ܪܫ
head	ܪܫܐ
chief	ܪܫܢܐ
wicked	ܪܫܝܥܐ
poll-tax	ܪܫܝܬܐ
mark	ܪܫܡ، ܪܫܡܐ
chief	ܪܫܢܐ
boil	ܪܬܚ، ܪܬܚܐ

ܫ

devil	ܫܐܕܐ
neighbor	ܫܒܒܐ
neighborhood	ܫܒܒܘܬܐ
proud	ܫܒܗܪܢܐ
glorify	ܫܒܚ، ܫܒܘܚܐ
February	ܫܒܛ
tribe	ܫܒܛܐ
glorius	ܫܒܝܚܐ
highway	ܫܒܝܠܐ
seventh	ܫܒܝܥܝܐ
bed	ܫܒܝܬܐ
window	ܫܒܟ
ear of corn	ܫܒܠܬܐ
seven	ܫܒܥܐ
seventy	ܫܒܥܝܢ
forgive, abandon	ܫܒܩ، ܫܒܩܐ
Saturday	ܫܒܬܐ

English	Chaldean	English	Chaldean
week	ܫ̄ܒܬ݂ܐ	shirt	ܫܘܩܢܐ
disturber	ܫ̇ܓܘܫܐ	jump	ܫܘܪܐ، ܫܘܪܬܐ
disturbance, tumult	ܫܓܘܫܝܐ	wall	ܫܘܪܐ
troubled	ܫܓܝܫܐ	soup	ܫܘܪܒܐ
shake	ܫܓܫ، ܫ̇ܓܘܫܐ	police	ܫܘܪܛܐ
pride	ܫܘܒܗܪܐ	beginning	ܫܘܪܝܐ
praise	ܫܘܒܚܐ	leap	ܫܘܪܬܐ
forgiveness	ܫܘܒܩܢܐ	bottle	ܫܝܫܐ
work, job	ܫܘܓܠܐ	lily	ܫܘܫܢܬܐ
let it be	ܫܘܕ	chalice veil	ܫܘܫܦܐ
alteration	ܫܘܚܠܦܐ	fellowship	ܫܘܬܦܘܬܐ
season	ܫܘܚܠܦܐ ܕܙܒܢܐ	charcoal	ܫܚܘܪܐ
scab	ܫܘܚܢܐ	warm	ܫܚܝܢܐ
bed	ܫܘܝܬܐ	vexed	ܫܚܝܩܐ
naked	ܫܘܠܚܐ	change	ܫܠܝܩ، ܫܠܘܩܐ
nakedness	ܫܘܠܚܝܘܬܐ	change	ܫܠܘܩܬܐ
authority	ܫܘܠܛܢܐ	warmth	ܫܚܝܢܘܬܐ
end	ܫܘܠܡܐ	snore	ܫܚܝܬܐ، ܫܚܢܬܐ
confirmation	ܫܘܡܠܝܐ	dirt	ܫܚܬܐ
torment	ܫܘܢܩܐ	stretch	ܫܛܚܐ، ܫܛܚ
place	ܫܘܦܐ	shepherd	ܫܒܝܢܐ
foot print	ܫܘܦܐ ܕܪܓܠܐ	insane	ܫܢܝܢܐ
beauty	ܫܘܦܪܐ	hades	ܫܝܘܠ
market	ܫܘܩܐ	peace, tranquility	ܫܝܢܐ
food store	ܫܘܩܐ ܕܙܘܒܠܬܐ		

139

pour	ܫܦܝܟ، ܫܦܟܐ
trumpet	ܫܝܦܘܪܐ
iron rod	ܫܝܫ
doubt	ܫܟ
ant	ܫܘܫܡܢܐ
picture	ܫܘܟܠܐ
picturesque	ܫܘܟܠܢܐ
sugar	ܫܟܪ
thank	ܫܟܝܪ، ܫܟܪܐ
be quiet	ܫܠܐ، ܫܠܝܐ
carcass	ܫܠܕܐ
furnace	ܫܠܘܚܝܬܐ
apostle	ܫܠܝܚܐ
apostolic	ܫܠܝܚܝܐ
ruler	ܫܠܝܛܐ
peace, hi, hello	ܫܠܡܐ
name	ܫܡܐ
watermelon	ܫܡܘܛܐ
take off	ܫܡܝܛ، ܫܡܛܐ
heaven	ܫܡܝܐ
heavenly	ܫܡܝܢܐ
loveliest	ܫܡܫܡܐ
hear	ܫܡܝܥ، ܫܡܥܐ
candle	ܫܡܥܐ
wax	ܫܡܥܐ
deacon	ܫܡܫܐ
sun	ܫܡܫܐ
solar	ܫܡܫܢܐ
sleep	ܫܢܬܐ
year	ܫܢܬܐ
yellow	ܫܥܘܬܐ
hour, clock, watch	ܫܥܬܐ
spill, overflow	ܫܦܝܥ، ܫܦܥܐ
beautiful	ܫܦܝܪܐ
beauty	ܫܦܝܪܘܬܐ، ܫܘܦܪܐ
supplicate	ܫܦܠܠ، ܫܦܠܘܠܐ
please	ܫܦܝܪ، ܫܦܪܐ
hat	ܫܦܩܐ
leg	ܫܩܐ
misery	ܫܩܝܘܬܐ
take	ܫܩܝܠ، ܫܩܠܐ
war, fight	ܫܪܐ
descend	ܫܪܝ، ܫܪܝܐ
lamp	ܫܪܓܐ
banquet	ܫܪܘܬܐ
company	ܫܪܝܟܘܬܐ
true	ܫܪܝܪܐ
truly	ܫܪܝܪܐܝܬ
beginning	ܫܘܪܝܬܐ

participate	ܫܵܬܸܦ، ܫܬܵܘܦܵܐ
remainder	ܫܪܵܟܵܐ
truth	ܫܪܵܪܵܐ
root	ܫܸܪܫܵܐ
chain	ܫܝܼܫܠܬܵܐ
sesame	ܫܝܼܫܡܵܐ
fever	ܫܲܚܬܵܐ
drink	ܫܬܹܐ، ܫܬܵܝܵܐ
foundation	ܫܬܵܐܣܬܵܐ
drink	ܫܬܝܼܬܵܐ
sixth	ܫܬܝܼܬܵܝܵܐ
seedling	ܫܬܸܠܵܐ
be silent	ܫܬܸܩ، ܫܬܵܩܵܐ
silence	ܫܬܵܩܵܐ
	ܬ
to, for	ܬܵܐ
wages	ܬܲܐܓܘܼܪܬܵܐ
fig	ܬܹܐܢܵܐ
broken	ܬܒܝܼܪܵܐ
break	ܬܒܸܪ، ܬܒܵܪܵܐ
merchant	ܬܲܓܵܪܵܐ
commerce	ܬܲܓܪܘܼܬܵܐ
class, division	ܬܸܓܡܵܐ
so that	ܬܵܕ
thank you	ܬܵܘܕܝ
confession, thanksgiving, religion	ܬܵܘܕܝܼܬܵܐ
education, discipline	ܬܘܼܠܡܵܕܵܐ
garlic	ܬܘܼܡܵܐ
date	ܬܘܼܡܪܵܐ
brown	ܬܘܼܡܪܵܢܵܐ
bull	ܬܵܘܪܵܐ
comment, interpretation	ܬܘܼܪܓܵܡܵܐ
cow	ܬܘܼܪܬܵܐ
mulberry	ܬܘܼܬܵܐ
new, recent	ܬܵܙܵܐ
fronteir, border, bound	ܬܚܘܼܡܵܐ
under; underneath	ܬܚܘܼܬ
plank	ܬܲܚܬܵܐ
penance, repentance	ܬܝܵܒܘܼܬܵܐ
repentance	ܬܝܵܒܘܼܬܵܐ
South	ܬܲܝܡܢܵܐ
urine	ܬܝܵܢܵܐ
hill	ܬܸܠܵܐ
refrigerator	ܬܲܠܓܵܝܵܐ
snow	ܬܲܠܓܵܐ
wet	ܬܲܠܝܼܠܵܐ
third	ܬܠܝܼܬܵܝܵܐ
Trinity	ܬܠܝܼܬܵܝܘܼܬܵܐ

disciple	ܬܲܠܡܝܼܕ݂ܵܐ
three	ܬܠܵܬ݂ܵܐ
Tuesday	ܬܠܵܬ݂ܒܫܲܒ݂ܵܐ
thirty	ܬܠܵܬ݂ܝܼܢ
thirteen	ܬܸܠܲܬ݂ܥܣܲܪ
there	ܬܲܡܵܐ
lazy	ܬܲܡܒܲܠ
why	ܬܲܡܘܿܗܵܐ، ܩܲܝ
July	ܬܲܡܘܼܙ
innocent	ܬܲܡܝܼܡܵܐ
eighth	ܬܡܝܼܢܵܝܵܐ
yesterday	ܬܸܡܵܠ
complete	ܬܲܡܵܡ
eight	ܬܡܵܢܝܵܐ
eighty	ܬܡܵܢܝܼܢ
eighteen	ܬܡܵܢܝܲܥܣܲܪ
repeat	ܬܵܢܹܐ، ܬܢܵܝܵܐ
oven	ܬܲܢܘܼܪܵܐ
groan	ܬܲܢܚܬܵܐ
dragon, serpent	ܬܲܢܝܼܢܵܐ
saying, word	ܬܲܢܝܼܬ݂ܵܐ
smoke	ܬܢܵܢܵܐ
skirt	ܬܲܢܢܘܼܪܵܐ
fox	ܬܲܥܠܵܐ
meet	ܬܵܦܹܩ، ܬܦܵܩܵܐ
weighed	ܬܩܝܼܠܵܐ
weigh	ܬܵܩܹܠ، ܬܩܵܠܵܐ
be wet	ܬܵܪܹܐ، ܬܪܵܝܵܐ
translate	ܬܲܪܓܸܡ، ܬܲܪܓܘܼܡܹܐ
altar	ܬܪܘܿܢܘܿܣ
two	ܬܪܹܝܢ
second	ܬܪܲܝܵܢܵܐ
Monday	ܬܪܹܝܢܒܫܲܒ݂ܵܐ
twelve	ܬܪܹܝܥܣܲܪ
door	ܬܲܪܥܵܐ
twelve Apostles	ܬܪܸܥܣܲܪܬܵܐ
praise	ܬܸܫܒܘܿܚܬܵܐ
ninth	ܬܫܝܼܥܵܝܵܐ
service	ܬܸܫܡܸܫܬܵܐ
nine	ܬܸܫܥܵܐ
ninety	ܬܸܫܥܝܼܢ
history	ܬܲܫܥܝܼܬ݂ܵܐ
nineteen	ܬܸܫܲܥܣܲܪ
October	ܬܸܫܪܝܼܢ ܐ
November	ܬܸܫܪܝܼܢ ܒ
fall (the season)	ܬܸܫܪܵܢܝܼܬܵܐ

Made in the USA
Monee, IL
04 October 2020